THE CHURCH AND THE NEGRO

THE CHURCH AND THE NEGRO

A Discussion of Mormons, Negroes and the Priesthood

by
JOHN LEWIS LUND

1967

This book is gratefully
dedicated to the author's
parents, Ilene L. Lund and
John J. Lund of Lacey,
Washington.

PREFACE

It is not the author's privilege, prerogative or intention to speak for The Church of Jesus Christ of Latter-day Saints, often referred to as the Mormon Church. This work must be regarded as the author's interpretation of research material found while examining the Mormon position concerning the Negro. Full responsibility is therefore assumed by the author for the contents of this book.

Much thought and consideration were given to the propriety of producing the following writing. It was for this reason that Church leaders in high positions were consulted. Although no official endorsement was sought, the author was encouraged to exercise his rights as an individual to publish this book.

ACKNOWLEDGMENTS

The author feels to express his most sincere gratitude to Bonnie Jeanne, his wife for the countless contributions she has made to this work. It can truly be said that without her encouragements and sacrifices this book would never have come to fruition.

The author also wishes to convey his appreciation to the Clearfield Seminary faculty and students of 1965 to 1967. In particular, Victor Judy, Ron Dent, Richards Durham, Merlyn Fowler, Douglas Keck and Dean Zimmerman are to be thanked for their wonderful lives which have served as an inspiration to the author.

Gratitude is also expressed to Dr. Melvin Petersen of Brigham Young University.

CONTENTS

I

INTRODUCTION

TODAY THE WORLD IS FILLED WITH CRIES OF SORROW. Tears of war strife, riot, poverty and confusion streak the face of our land. It is a time of frustration for many citizens, whether black, brown, yellow, red or white. It is a time when some shout phrases like "God is dead!" and "Where is justice?" Newspaper headlines are filled with daily disasters, and Despair seems to be raising her ugly head as the ruler of our time.

Amid this confusion and turmoil the civil rights movement is emerging as the dragon slayer of certain social evils. The dragons of prejudice and discrimination are being attacked, and rightly so, by many of those who believe in the dignity of the human soul. Equality, justice and individual rights are being demanded for all. And, as is the case in most struggles, a few innocent casualties are to be expected and summarily excused; but there is no excuse for attacking the innocent in the name of might or right. There are some who say they are fighting for basic freedoms and so they swing their swords of social pressure and law at any and all who appear to differ in the least from what they believe. The civil rights cause is just and few question its basic precepts. The methods, however, are occasionally questionable and the dragon is sometimes a dove that is attacked and wounded in the heat of emotional excitement.

The Mormon Church has been attacked as one that discriminates against the Negroes in the community. Nothing could be further from the truth. The Mormon religion is a voice that offers peace to a war-torn world, peace of mind, of body and of spirit. It offers faith to black and white alike in a world that doubts God's existence. The church asks the question, "Is there any greater cure for the sicknesses of the world than the Gospel of

Jesus Christ?" It answers, "No!" The Gospel is the message that Mormons bear. The Church teaches that the Gospel encompasses those of all races. Every man, woman and child that ever lived on the face of this earth is a beloved child of a kind Father in Heaven, a God that is not a respecter of persons. His Church extends to all the hand of friendship and fellowship. The call to repentance is not made to white alone, but to black as well, for all have need of repentance. Baptism is offered to all who desire to follow Christ, the greatest civil rights leader of all. Christ has said that His law is encompassed in the commandments of love of God and love of fellowman. This is what The Church of Jesus Christ of Latter-day Saints, commonly called the Mormon Church, believes.

This book is written for the express purpose of explaining to the members of The Church of Jesus Christ of Latter-day Saints the doctrine of the Church concerning the Negro. It is expected that many non-Mormons as well as Negroes will read this work. It is hoped that all who do will be open-minded and fair in their evaluation of the Mormon position.

When the reader has finished with this brief explanation, he may find that he does not agree with the opinions herein expressed. That is his right. But the author and the Church are also entitled to their right of believing as they will and following the dictates of their own consciences. As one wise man once said, "Your right to swing your fist ends where my nose begins." Whether a person wants to swing his fist for civil rights or in the name of justice, morality, human dignity, freedom, liberty, equality or God, his rights end where another's begin. In other words, the Church believes that all have a right to enjoy their individual freedoms as long as they do not prevent others from enjoying their rights.

It is the most ardent desire of the author that even those who do not agree with the Mormon position will at least understand why Latter-day Saints believe as they do.

II

A WORD ABOUT DISCRIMINATION

THE CHURCH BELIEVES THAT NO MAN HAS THE RIGHT TO treat his neighbor—regardless of race, color, or creed—with any less respect than he would treat Jesus Christ Himself. For every injustice or unrighteous discrimination a man will be called before the bar of God to answer for his deeds. The Savior taught, "Inasmuch as ye have done it unto one of the least of these my brethren, ye have done it unto me."[1] If any person, because of wealth, pride, social position or race looks down on any member of the human family, he is guilty of a serious sin.

As previously mentioned in the introduction, all men and women are sons and daughters of a loving Father in Heaven. This infers that all are brothers and sisters regardless of race and should be treated as such. There was only one race in Heaven before we came to this earth. As Paul has said, ". . . God . . . hath made of one blood all nations of men to dwell on all the face of the earth . . ."[2] After every man has died and received his resurrection there will once again be a single race. However, God has ordained that for this mortal existence there be many races and He has also commanded that these races treat one another as brothers.

Certainly there are those members in the Church who are guilty of unrighteous discrimination. Nevertheless, no intelligent person would assume that the personality quirks, likes or dislikes of the individual members comprise the official doctrine of the Church. If a man is found who discriminates unrighteously, whether Catholic, Jew, Protestant or Mormon, then lay the charge of discrimination at his feet. It would be a mistake to condemn any church because of the individual prejudices of its members. One might properly inquire as to whether the church is succeeding in influencing the individual who discriminates, but one must never condemn the religious organization because it has an imperfect member.

The goal of the LDS Church is perfection for each and every person, but the Church makes no claim to having all perfect members. Those who would judge the doctrine of the Church by the acts of individual members should be careful that they do not fall into the trap of unsound reasoning:

> I saw a Catholic who hated his neighbor.
> Therefore, all Catholics hate their neighbors.
> Therefore, the Catholic Church teaches, "Hate thy neighbor!"

or

> I saw a Mormon who liked to smoke cigars.
> Therefore, all Mormons like to smoke cigars.
> Therefore, the Mormon Church teaches its members to smoke cigars.

Ridiculous is a word that describes this particular type of reasoning. Yet, there are many who use such generalizations apparently ignorant of the logic they are utilizing.

Christ taught love of fellowmen, of all men. It is His injunction that each man treat his neighbor as he himself would want to be treated.[3] As followers of Christ, Mormons believe in obeying this Golden Rule in dealing with any individual regardless of race.

How Are All Man Created Equal?

As Christ indicated in the parable of the talents, to each a different talent is given; some may receive many while others receive but a few.[4] This parable suggests that all men are not born with the same talents, abilities or opportunities. It is true that all men stand equal before God in the fact that they will be judged in the use of their free agency. It is doubtful, however, that any serious observer would say that all men are equal as far as social, economic or intellectual capacities are concerned. As stated by an early apostle in the Church, "In the first place, if all men were created alike, if all had the same degree of intelligence and purity of disposition, all would be equal. But, notwithstanding the declaration of the . . . Fathers of our country to the contrary, it is a fact that all beings are not equal in their intellectual capacity, in their dispositions, and in the gifts and callings of God. . . . some beings are more intelligent than others, and some are endowed with abilities or gifts which others do not possess."[5]

In a letter from the First Presidency of the Church on this subject to Dr. Lowry Nelson, the following statement was issued:

> The basic element of your ideas and concepts seems to be that all God's children stand in equal positions before Him in all things.
>
> Your knowledge of the Gospel will indicate to you that that this is contrary to the very fundamentals of God's dealing with Israel dating from the time of His promise to Abraham regarding Abraham's seed and their position vis-a-vis with God Himself. Indeed, some of God's children were assigned to superior positions before the world was formed. We are aware that some higher critics do not accept this, but the Church does.[6]

How then are all men created equal? They are created equal in two respects. All men are born innocent before God and should be equal before the law. What about the Negro? ". . . like all other spirits who come into this world, they are innocent before God so far as mortal existence is concerned . . . If they prove faithful in this estate, without doubt, our Eternal Father, who is just and true, will reward them accordingly and there will be in store for them some blessings of exaltation."[7] God treats all men as individuals in the use of their free agency. He gives every man the opportunity to attain the highest Celestial goals. The factor that determines whether or not the individual attains these goals is dependent solely upon his own efforts.

Equal Before the Law

Mormons are firm in their belief that the Negro is

entitled to every right guaranteed by our constitution. President Joseph Fielding Smith has said,

> No church or other organization is more insistent than The Church of Jesus Christ of Latter-day Saints, that the Negroes should receive all the rights and privileges that can possibly be given to any other in the true sense of equality as declared in the *Declaration of Independence.* They should be equal to "life, liberty, and the pursuit of happiness." They should be equal in the matter of education. They should not be barred from obtaining knowledge and becoming proficient in any field of science, art or mechanical occupation. They should be free to choose any kind of employment, to go into business in any field they may choose and to make their lives as happy as it is possible without interference from white, labor unions or from any other source. In their defense of these privileges the members of the Church will stand.[8]

Does the Mormon Church discriminate against the Negro? The answer is, "No!!" The official Church position is that Negroes are sons and daughters of God and may through righteous works and faith return to His presence. Individual Church members who unrighteously discriminate against the Negro should be warned that they are not in harmony with the Gospel of Jesus Christ.

FOOTNOTES

[1]Matt. 25:40, King James.

[2]Acts 17:24-26, King James.

[3]Matt. 7:12, King James.

[4]Matt. 25:24-26, King James.

[5]Parley P. Pratt, *Journal of Discourses,* (Lithographic reprint of original; Liverpool: S. W. Richards, 1964), p. 257.

[6]John J. Stewart, *Mormonism and the Negro* (Orem, Utah: Bookmark Division of Community Press Publishing Company, 1960), p. 46.

[7]Joseph Fielding Smith, *The Way to Perfection* (eleventh edition; Salt Lake City, Utah: Genealogical Society of The Church of Jesus Christ of Latter-day Saints, 1958), pp. 43-44.

[8]Joseph Fielding Smith, *Answers to Gospel Questions* (Salt Lake City, Utah: Deseret Book Company, 1958), 2:185.

III

DAVID O. McKAY'S
STATEMENT ON THE NEGRO

DAVID O. McKAY, THE PROPHET, SEER AND REVELATOR of The Church of Jesus Christ of Latter-day Saints, made a statement in 1947 concerning the Negro which represents the feelings of the Mormon Church toward this group. The Prophet said, "George Washington Carver was one of the noblest souls that ever came to earth. He held a close kinship with his Heavenly Father, and rendered a service to his fellow men such as few have ever excelled."[9] He went on to include those of all races when he said, "For every righteous endeavor, for every noble impulse, for every good deed performed in his useful life, George Washington Carver will be rewarded, and so will every other man, be he red, white, black or yellow, for God is no respecter of persons."[10]

The statement just quoted by our prophet communicates more than any other the Mormon position on the Negro. The Church does not support social discriminations in any way, shape or form against any group in the world. It calls all to repentance. It preaches the necessity of baptism for all who would accept Christianity. It offers principles of faith and righteous living that can be embraced by all those who desire to accept Jesus Christ as their personal Savior.

Mormons believe that the Celestial Kingdom where God and the righteous dwell will be filled with the worthy sons and daughters of God from all races, including noble Negroes who hold high Christian ideals of love of God and love of fellow man.

FOOTNOTES

[9]William E. Berrett, "The Church and the Negroid People," *Mormonism and the Negro, op. cit.,* p. 23.
[10]*Ibid.*

IV

HOW DOES THE STORY OF CAIN RELATE TO THE NEGRO?

IT IS AT THIS POINT THAT THE BIBLICAL AND THEOLOGI-cal foundations of Mormon doctrine must be examined as they relate to Cain. This will be done by analyzing in some detail the story of Cain.

King James Version: (Gen. 4)[11]

1. And Adam knew Eve his wife; and she conceived, and bare Cain, and said, I have gotten a man from the Lord.

2. And she again bare his brother Abel. And Abel was a keeper of sheep, but Cain was a tiller of the ground.

3. And in process of time it came to pass, that Cain brought of the fruit of the ground an offering unto the Lord.

4. And Abel, he also brought of the firstlings of his flock and of the fat thereof. And the Lord had respect unto Abel and to his offering:

The Inspired Version: (Gen. 5)[12]

4. And Adam knew Eve his wife, and she conceived and bare Cain, and said, I have gotten a man from the Lord; wherefore he may not reject his words. But, behold, also Cain hearkened not, saying, Who is the Lord, that I should know him?

5. And she again conceived, and bare his brother Abel. And Abel hearkened unto the voice of the Lord. And Abel was a keeper of sheep, but Cain was a tiller of the ground.

6. And Cain Loved Satan more than God. And Satan commanded him, saying, Make an offering unto the Lord. And in process of time it came to pass, that Cain brought of the fruit of the ground an offering unto the Lord.

7. And Abel, he also brought, of the firstlings of his flock, and of the fat thereof; and the Lord had respect unto Abel, and to his offering, but unto

Cain, and to his offering, he had not respect.

5. But unto Cain and to his offering he had not respect. And Cain was very wroth, and his countenance fell.

6. And the Lord said unto Cain, why art thou wroth? and why is thy countenance fallen?

7. If thou doest well, shalt thou not be accepted? and if thou doest not well, sin lieth at the door. And unto thee shall be his desire, and thou shalt rule over him.

8. Now Satan knew this, and it pleased him. And Cain was very wroth, and his countenance fell.

9. And the Lord said unto Cain, Why art thou wroth? Why is thy countenance fallen? If thou doest well thou shalt be accepted, and if thou doest not well, sin lieth at the door; and Satan desireth to have thee, and except thou shalt hearken unto my commandments, I will deliver thee up, and it shall be unto thee according to his desire; and thou shalt rule over him, for from this time forth thou shalt be the father of his lies.

10. Thou shalt be called Perdition, for thou wast also before the world, and it shall be said in time to come, that these abominations were had from Cain, for he rejected the greater counsel, which was had from God; and this is a cursing which I will put upon thee, except thou repent.

11. And Cain was wroth, and listened not any more to the voice of the Lord, neither to Abel his brother, who walked in holiness before the Lord.

12. And Adam also, and his wife, mourned before the Lord, because of Cain and his brethren.

13. And it came to pass, that Cain took one of his brother's daughters to wife, and they loved Satan more than God.

14. And Satan said unto Cain, Swear unto me by thy throat, and if thou tell it thou shalt die; and swear thy brethren by their heads, and by the living God, that they tell it not; for if they tell it they shall surely die; and this that thy father may not know it; and this day I will deliver thy brother Abel into thine hands.

15. And Satan swear unto Cain, that he would do according to his commands. And all these things were done in secret.

16. And Cain said, Truly I am Mahan, the master of this great secret, that I may murder and get gain. Wherefore Cain was called Master Mahan; and he gloried in his wickedness.

8. And Cain talked with Abel his brother: and it came to pass, when they were in the field, that Cain rose up against Abel his brother, and slew him.

17. And Cain went into the field, and Cain talked with Abel his brother; and it came to pass, that while they were in the field, Cain rose up against Abel his brother, and slew him.

18. And Cain gloried in that which he had done, saying, I am free; surely the flocks of my brother falleth into my hands.

9. And the Lord said unto Cain, Where is Abel thy brother? And he said, I know not: Am I my brother's keeper?

19. And the Lord said unto Cain, Where is Abel, thy brother? And he said, I know not, am I my brother's keeper?

10. And he said, What hast thou done? the voice of thy

20. And the Lord said, What hast thou done? The voice of

brother's blood crieth unto me from the ground.

11. And now art thou cursed from the earth, which hath opened her mouth to receive thy brother's blood from thy hand;

12. When thou tillest the ground, it shall not henceforth yield unto thee her strength; a fugitive and a vagabond shalt thou be in the earth.

13. And Cain said unto the Lord, My punishment is greater than I can bear.

14. Behold, thou hast driven met out this day from the face of the earth; and from thy face shall I be hid; and I shall be a fugitive and a vagabond in the earth; and it shall come to pass, that every one that findeth me shall slay me.

15. And the Lord said unto him, Therefore whosoever slayeth Cain, vengeance shall be taken on him sevenfold. And the Lord set a mark upon Cain, lest any finding him should kill me.

16. And Cain went out from the presence of the Lord, and dwelt in the land of Nod, on the east of Eden.

thy brother's blood cries unto me from the ground.

21. And now, thou shalt be cursed from the earth, which hath opened her mouth to receive thy brother's blood from thy hand.

22. When thou tillest the ground, it shall not henceforth yield unto thee her strength; a fugitive and a vagabond shalt thou be in the earth.

23. And Cain said unto the Lord, Satan tempted me, because of my brother's flock; and I was wroth also, for his offering thou didst accept, and not mine.

24. My punishment is greater than I can bear. Behold, thou hast driven me out this day from the face of the Lord, and from thy face shall I be hid; and I shall be a fugitive and a vagabond in the earth; and it shall come to pass, that he that findeth me shall slay me, because of mine iniquities, for these things are not hid from the Lord.

25. And I, the Lord, said unto him, Whosoever slayeth thee, vengeance shall be taken on him seven-fold; and I, the Lord, set a mark upon Cain, lest any finding him should kill him.

26. And Cain was shut out from the presence of the Lord, and with his wife and many of his brethren, dwelt in the land of Nod, on the east of Eden.

17. And Cain knew his wife; and she conceived, and bare Enoch; and he builded a city, and called the name of the city, after the name of his son, Enoch.

27. And Cain knew his wife, and she conceived and bare Enoch, and he also begat many sons and daughters. And he builded a city, and he called the name of the city after the name of his son Enoch.

WHAT WAS THE MARK OF CAIN?

THE BIBLICAL SCHOLARS OF THE WORLD ARE AT GREAT variance as to what exactly was the mark of Cain. The phrase "set a mark upon"[13] is mentioned only twice in the entire Bible. Both of these references are found in the Old Testament. The first is in Genesis 4:15, "The Lord set a mark upon Cain lest any finding him should kill him." The other reference is located in Ezekiel 9:4, which states "set a mark upon the foreheads of the men." It is immediately apparent because of the identical wording that many students of the Bible would be persuaded to believe that the marks were similar, if not identical, in both cases. Thus, we have the first opinion as to what the mark of Cain was. "The mark of Cain was, perhaps a tattoo . . ."[14] "What this sign was is not known specifically; possibly the best suggestion is that it was a tribal sign, like the tattooed 'wasm' frequently found among the Bedouins."[15] It is the opinion of these and countless other scholars that the mark of Cain was some type of marking on the forehead. In movies and filmstrips of the Cain and Abel story, the mark of Cain is regularly represented as a wide line across the forehead.[16] Such assumptions are grossly careless, yet understandable when one considers the lack of inspiration.

Another opinion as to the mark of Cain is equally uninspired yet considerably more scholarly. A close examination of the Hebrew text in Genesis 4:15 and Ezekiel 9:4 is quite revealing. In Ezekiel the Hebrew word used for mark is תָּו or TAV, which literally means "a mark." On the other hand, the word in the Hebrew text in Genesis is אות or OTH which does not mean mark at all but rather "a sign."[17] Therefore a sign was given unto Cain. Such scholars as Shuckford are of the opinion that God gave a sign unto Cain, "not . . . by setting a mark upon him, which is a false translation, but by appointing a sign or token which he himself might understand . . ."[18]

There are some scholars who will not commit themselves fully, yet maintain that "God marked him [Cain] with some visible token."[19] Dr. J. Hastings believes that "by the sign has been understood a miracle which in the time of need might terrify an assailant, e.g.; but the idea rather appears to be that a permanent physical brand was imprinted . . ."[20] Upon going to the Hebrew it was found that the word used in Genesis 4:15 for mark was actually a combination of the previous ideas and opinions given. James Strong, S.T.D., LL.D., in his *Hebrew and Chaldee Dictionary*, gives the following definition to the Hebrew word:

> " אות 'owth or oth in the sense of appearing, a signal, mark, or sign."[21]

Using Bible sources and Bible scholars alone it is significantly evident that a clear majority believe that a permanent signal, mark, or sign appeared on Cain. Fortunately, the LDS scholar does not have to rely on Bible sources alone. The Standard Works of the Church, plus the inspirations of the living oracles of God, have given us great insight and answers to many religious questions, not solely the issue of the mark of Cain. On the subject of the mark of Cain our prophets have given all the important information that is necessary to our salvation. Frankly, sincerely, and somewhat abruptly, President Brigham Young has told us that the mark of Cain was a "black skin."[22] For the Latter-day Saint no further explanation is required. However, it is not necessary to rely on this single statement to arrive at this same conclusion. There are numerous references made by both ancient and modern prophets that point to the fact that Cain was the father of the race that became known as Negroid.

The fact that Cain was black does not of itself prove that all of his descendants were black. It is conceivable, as some have argued, that the Lord marked Cain with a black skin and at the same time removed the mark from his descendants. This issue might be of considerable merit were it not for the revealed truth that has come through the Lord's prophets. "And Enoch also beheld the residue of the people which were the sons of Adam; and they were a mixture of all the seed of Adam save it was the seed of Cain, for the seed of Cain were black, and had not place among them."[23] Wilford Woodruff taught that "the Lord said I will not kill Cain, but I will put a mark upon him, and that mark will be seen upon the face of every Negro upon the face of the earth . . ."[24] The question as to what the mark of Cain was, and is, is thus answered—a black skin for him and his posterity.

WHY DID CAIN RECEIVE THE MARK?

HAVING IDENTIFIED THE MARK OF CAIN, WE MUST NEXT address ourselves to the question, "Why was the mark or sign placed on Cain?" On this point the Bible scholars appear almost united. The mark set upon Cain was given as a sign of protection. It was pronounced after a plea from Cain. In his own words, "Behold, thou hast driven me out this day from the face of the Earth; and it shall come to pass that everyone that find me shall slay me."[25] Therefore, the Lord marked Cain with a black skin so that all would know and recognize Cain on sight "lest any finding him should kill him."[26] Dummelow in his Bible commentary claims, "Perhaps it was some token to assure him safety, like the rainbow at the flood. Others take it that Cain was marked in some way to show that he was under God's protection."[27] Hartman of the Catholic school believes, "He was shielded against blood vengeance by a sign placed on him by Yahweh."[28] Students of the Revised Standard Version make the allegation that "the mark of Cain was a protective mark . . ."[29] Fallow's Bible Encyclopedia reiterates that Cain was cursed ". . . but he was to be protected against the wrath of his fellowmen: and of this God gave him assurance."[30] J. Hastings asserts that, "Afraid for his life, which he feels to be forfeited [Cain] is vouchsafed the protection of the threat of a sevenfold vengeance and of a special sign."[31] The mark of a black skin was not "the curse" as some have supposed, but a sign of protection given to Cain.

A second reason for the mark of a black skin deals specifically with the problems of intermarriage. The Lord did not want the seed of Cain to intermingle with the rest of Adam's children. The reasons will be discussed under the heading "Interracial Marriage and the Negro."

WHAT WAS THE CURSE OF CAIN?

THE CURSE THAT ACCOMPANIED THE MARK IS THE TOPIC of proximate interest. "To curse, signifies to imprecate, to call for mischief upon, or wish evil to anyone. God pronounced his curse against . . . Cain, who had imbued his hands in his brother's blood. The divine maledictions are not merely imprecations, nor are they impotent wishes; but they carry their effects with them, and are attended with all the miseries they pronounce or foretell."[32] The אָרַר (arar)[33] or curse that Cain brought upon himself is far more profound than a simple reading of the Biblical account would render. "And now art thou cursed from the earth . . . , when thou tillest the ground it shall not henceforth yield unto thee her strength; a fugitive and a vagabond shalt thou be in the earth."[34]

Cain was assured by God of protection. He had his life. In fact, later he married and founded a city, citizened by his followers.[35] What would occasion Cain to exclaim to the Lord, "My punishment is greater than I can bear."?[36] It is this passage more than any other that gives an insight into the nature of Cain's curse. Another translation of the foregoing phrase is, "Mine iniquity is greater than that it may be forgiven."[37]

Cain's Curse—A Son of Perdition

At this point the LDS scholar must leave the Bible as a sole reference and turn to the other sources of revealed truth. In the *Doctrine and Covenants* we read, "The blasphemy against the Holy Ghost, which shall not be forgiven in the world nor out of the world, is in that ye commit murder wherein ye shed innocent blood, and assent unto my death, after ye have received my new and everlasting covenant, saith the Lord God."[38] The Prophet Joseph Smith tells us:

> All sins shall be forgiven, except the sin against the Holy Ghost; for Jesus will save all except the sons of perdition. What must a man do to commit the unpardonable sin? He must receive the Holy Ghost, have the heavens opened unto him, and know God, and then sin against Him. After a man has sinned against the Holy Ghost, there is no repentance for him. "For it is impossible for those who were once enlightened, and have tasted of the heavenly gift, and were made partakers of the Holy Ghost, and have tasted the good word of God, and the powers of the world to come, if they shall fall away, to renew them again unto repentance; seeing they crucify to themselves the Son of God afresh, and put him to an open shame." (Heb. 6:4-6). Those who sin against the light and knowledge of the Holy Ghost may be said to crucify more than the body of our Lord, they crucify the Spirit. He has got to say that the sun does not shine while he sees it; he has got to deny the plan of salvation with his eyes open to the truth of it; and from that time he begins to be an enemy.[39]

Cain qualified for the foregoing definition in that he was instructed by Father Adam in all things of the Gospel.[40] Cain had accepted the new and everlasting covenant, which is the Gospel.[41] "He understood the Gospel and the plan of salvation, was baptized, received the Priesthood, had a perfect knowledge of the position and perfection of God, and talked personally with Deity."[42] The murder of Abel was no accident. Neither could it be classified as a passion murder. Cain might have been angry when he rose up and slew Abel, but the murder was cold-blooded, premeditated, and would be classified today as first degree.

The scriptures tell us that "Cain loved Satan more than God."[43] Had Cain been on earth when the Savior was here he would have consented to, if not actually taken part in, the murder of Jesus Christ even though he knew that Christ was truly the Son of God. It is little wonder that God said to Cain, "For thou wast [Perdition] also before the world."[44] The punishment that was greater than he could bear was very probably the knowledge that he was a Son of Perdition. *The Book of Mormon* states that Cain was "a murderer from the beginning."[45] Joseph Fielding Smith has declared that "He sinned against the light; otherwise his sin could not make of him Perdition."[46] Evidently the Lord revealed unto Cain the plight which is known only to those who make of themselves Sons of Perdition. "Wherefore, He saves all except them—they shall go away into everlasting punishment, which is endless punishment, which is eternal punishment, to reign with the devil and his angels in eternity, where their worm dieth not, and the fire is not quenched, which is their torment—and the end thereof, neither the place thereof, nor their torment, NO MAN KNOWS; neither was it revealed, neither is, neither will be revealed unto man, EXCEPT TO THEM WHO ARE MADE PARTAKERS THEREOF."[47] What "hell" must await Cain knowing that he has still to face God in that last judgment and hear Him say, "Depart ye cursed," as stated in the *Doctrine and Covenants* 29:41.

It has been pointed out that the mark of Cain was a black skin and that he received it as a symbol of protection. The curse of Cain was that of a Son of Perdition with its accompanying loss of Priesthood, and damnation.

WHAT WAS THE SEVEN-FOLD VENGEANCE

WHY WOULD THE LORD ANNOUNCE THAT A SEVEN-FOLD vengeance would be taken on anyone who might slay Cain?[48] Certainly Cain was worthy of death. "Whoso sheddeth man's blood, by man shall his blood be shed."[49]

Why would the Lord say, "I will not kill Cain . . ."[50]
What would occasion Him to make an exception in his
case? Is it possible that the Lord had a purpose for not
shedding the blood of Cain? If so, what was that purpose?

By becoming a Son of Perdition Cain was cursed in
that he could no longer have the Priesthood. He was also
set apart by the Lord to become the father of the Negroid
race. It was through Cain that those who were not to
receive the Priesthood during their mortal existence were
to come. It should be emphasized that the Lord did not
arbitrarily choose Cain. Cain, using his free agency, chose
to "love Satan more than God." Cain had no one but
himself to blame for being a Son of Perdition. Did not
God tell him, "If thou doest well shalt thou not be accepted?"[51] Having lost his rights and privileges to serve
the Lord, Cain was still to be an instrument in bringing
about the purposes of the Lord.

Had the blood of Cain been shed, the plan of God to
send the non-Priesthood holders through his lineage would
have been frustrated.[52] Therefore, the Lord announced
that a seven-fold vengeance would be taken on the man
who slew Cain. We can only suppose what this vengeance might have been. It is very possible that the man
who might have slain Cain would have had to replace
Cain as the progenitor of those who were not to receive
the Priesthood in this life. This is pure conjecture on the
part of the author and should not be interpreted as official
Church doctrine concerning the seven-fold vengeance.

A common misconception concerning the seven-fold
vengeance is that if one kills a Negro descendant of Cain,
the slayer takes upon himself the seven-fold vengeance
pronounced by the Lord. In view of the previous explanation this idea would certainly be erroneous.

WHY DID THE LORD
REJECT CAIN'S OFFERING?

CAIN MADE AN IMPORTANT DECISION IN THE OFFERING
that he made to the Lord.[53] In order to understand

the issues involved with the offering, it becomes necessary to make a closer examination of the story of Cain. Why would the Lord reject Cain's offering? There appear to be two fundamental reasons why the Lord would not accept the offering. First, it was inappropriate; second, it was inspired by Satan.

Cain's Offering—A Rejection of the Atonement

The Biblical scholars in general are in the dark as far as this question is concerned. It is amazing, however, how close the following account is to the correct principles:

> It is not stated why the Lord had no regard for Cain and his offering. The same silence may have marked the legend in its original form before it was adapted to its present context. It is possible, however, that a reason was there given, and that its omission was a piece of ptolemaic against the peasant custom of bringing the fruit of the ground as an offering to the Lord, instead of the time-honored nomad offering of an animal.[54]

The foregoing, although somewhat ambiguous, is very close to what Charles W. Penrose stated in clearer terms in May of 1883:

> When Abel would worship God in the way appointed, Cain who wanted to go his own way, offered what he pleased, what he thought would do, and he was filled with anger towards Abel because his offering was accepted. Abel offered what God commanded, the firstlings of the flock. Cain offered the fruits of the ground. God had commanded a lamb without blemish and without spot, to be offered as an emblem of the coming Redeemer who in the meridian of time should come as "The Lamb slain from before the foundation of the world," and offer His life and pour out His blood for the remission of sins. Cain offered what he pleased and when Abel's offering was accepted Cain was filled with anger. The spirit of Satan entered into him— which is the spirit of destruction, the spirit of murder—and he arose and slew his brother.[55]

Cain held the Holy Priesthood. Otherwise he would not have had the responsibility or opportunity of making an offering. The Lord did not reject Cain because of an

unauthorized offering such as Saul made.[56] This point,
although apparently small, is of the greatest significance.
Saul made an offering unto the Lord without authority and
therefore was rejected by the Lord.[57] Cain had the
authority to make a proper offering, but was rejected for
a different reason. The Lord recognized Cain's Priesthood
when He said, "If thou doest well, shalt thou not be
accepted?"[58]

One of the primary commandments of God to Adam,
Eve, and their children was to "offer the firstlings of their
flocks."[59] No mention was made of any other type of
offering for the purpose of remembering the Atonement of
Jesus Christ. Fruits of the ground were often accepted as
tithes or other types of offerings,[60] but not to be confused with the symbolic offering of an animal. The reason
the Lord wanted the firstlings of the flock was, as the
angel said to Adam, "This thing is a similitude of the sacrifice of the Only Begotten of the Father, which is full of
grace and truth."[61] Cain, by offering the fruits of the
ground, was in reality rejecting, not only Jesus Christ, but
also the Atonement.

> By faith in this atonement or plan of redemption, Abel
> offered to God a sacrifice that was accepted, which was the
> firstlings of the flock. Cain offered of the fruit of the ground,
> and was not accepted, because he could not do it in faith [of
> the Atonement], he could have no faith, or could not exercise
> faith contrary to the plan of heaven. It must be shedding the
> blood of the Only Begotten to atone for man; for this was
> the plan of redemption, and without the shedding of blood
> was no remission; and as the sacrifice was instituted for a
> type, by which man was to discern the great Sacrifice which
> God had prepared; to offer a sacrifice contrary to that, no
> faith [in the Atonement] could be exercised, because redemp-
> tion was not purchased in that way, nor the power of
> atonement instituted after that order; consequently Cain
> could have no faith; and whatsoever is not of faith, is sin.
> But Abel offered an acceptable sacrifice, by which he ob-
> tained witness that he was righteous, God Himself testifying
> of his gifts. Certainly, the shedding of the blood of a beast
> could be beneficial to no man, except it was done in imi-
> tation, or as a type, or explanation of what was to be of-

fered through the gift of God Himself; and this performance done with an eye looking forward in faith on the power of that great Sacrifice for a remission of sins. But however various may have been, and may be at the present time, the opinions of men respecting the conduct of Abel, and the knowledge which he had on the subject of atonement, it is evident in our minds, that he was instructed more fully in the plan than what the Bible speaks of, for how could he offer a sacrifice in faith, looking to God for a remission of his sins in the power of the great atonement, without having been previously instructed in that plan? And further, if he was accepted of God, what were the ordinances performed besides the offering of the firstlings of the flock?

It is said by Paul in his letter to the Hebrew brethren, that Abel obtained witness that he was righteous, God testifying of his gifts. To whom did God testify of the gifts of Abel, was it to Paul? We have very little on this important subject in the forepart of the Bible, but is said that Abel himself obtained witness that he was righteous. Then certainly God spoke to him: and if He did, would He not, seeing that Abel was righteous, deliver to him the whole plan of the Gospel. And is not the Gospel the news of the redemption? How could Abel offer a sacrifice and look forward with faith on the Son of God for a remission of his sins, and not understand the Gospel? The mere shedding of the blood of beasts or offering anything else in sacrifice, could not procure a remission of sins, except it were performed in faith of something to come; if it could, Cain's offering must have been as good as Abel's.[62]

Therefore, the Lord rejected the offering of Cain in that it was improper, unsuited, and thereby unworthy by all standards of that which the Lord had requested.

Cain's Offering—Satan Inspired

The other basic reason for the Lord's rejection lies in the fact that it was Satan inspired. "And Cain loved Satan more than God. And Satan commanded him saying, Make an offering unto the Lord. And in the process of time, it came to pass, that Cain brought of the fruit of the ground an offering unto the Lord."[63] It becomes quite understandable why the Lord would reject Cain's offering. That which is difficult to understand is Cain's somewhat surprised reaction to an obvious response from the Lord.

WHY DID CAIN KILL ABEL?

GERMANE TO THE ENTIRE STORY OF CAIN IS THE QUES-
tion of Abel's murder. In pleading his case before
the Lord, Cain gave three reasons for his infamous deed.
First, he calimed, "Satan tempted me";[64] secondly, he admitted a desire to possess his "brother's flocks,"[65] and
thirdly, he stated, "I was wroth also, for his offering thou
didst accept, and not mine."[66] A brief examination of each
of the reasons offered in Cain's confession will reveal a
motive far more profound than a simple reading of the
account would render.

"Satan Tempted Me"

The temptation that Cain considered so great arose in
the form of a covenant. It was with Satan that Cain made
an agreement to slay Abel. What was the significance of
the covenant that Cain made with Satan? As with any
covenant or contract, the parties involved must agree to
the terms. It is written that Cain agreed to kill his brother
Abel. What was Satan's part of the contract? "And Satan
swear unto Cain, that he would do according to his commands."[67] Is one to understand from this that Cain will
rule over Satan?

In order to answer this question it becomes necessary
to re-examine the Lord's warning to Cain if he refused to
hearken unto the commandments of God: ". . . and if
thou doest not well, sin lieth at the door; and Satan desireth to have thee, and except thou shalt hearken unto my
commandments, I will deliver thee up, and it shall be
unto thee according to his [Satan's] desire; and THOU
[Cain] shalt rule over him [Satan], for from this time forth
thou shalt be the father of his lies. Thou shalt be called
Perdition, for thou wast also before the world, and it shall
be said in time to come, that these abominations were had
from Cain . . ."[68]

In the King James Version this same story is told.
"And unto thee [Cain] shall be his [Satan's] desire and
thou [Cain] shalt rule over him [Satan]."[69] This then was

a part of the contract Satan made with Cain. This was the great temptation. In the eternities to come Cain will rule over Satan. "As a result of his mortal birth he [Cain] is assured of a tangible body of flesh and bones in eternity, a fact which will enable him to rule over Satan."[70] Joseph Fielding Smith tells us that "Satan wanted him because Cain had a body. He wanted more power. A man with a body, of course, will have greater power than just a spirit without a body."[71]

The other part of the covenant that Satan made with Cain was that if he would slay Abel, Satan would establish with him "secret oaths and covenants."[72] The purpose of these secret oaths and covenants would be "to gain power, and to murder, and to plunder, and to lie, and to commit all manner of wickedness and whoredoms."[73] "And Cain said, truely I am Mahan, the master of the great secret, that I may murder and get gain. Wherefore Cain was called Master Mahan; and he gloried in his wickedness."[74] Cain covenanted to kill Abel and Satan agreed to be subject to Cain in the eternities. In his new role as Master Mahan, Cain's first official act was to murder Abel. From that time forth Cain became the Father of all wickedness.

It is undeniably true that Satan tempted Cain; but, he also tempted the rest of the sons and daughters of Adam and Eve. Cain would have one believe that he gave in to Satan's temptation because he did not know any better. It is written, however, that "Adam and Even blessed the name of God; and they made all things known unto their sons and their daughters."[75] Cain committed the murder of Abel with a full perspective of what was right and what was wrong. When Adam instructed Cain in the commandments of God, he replied, "Who is the Lord, that I should know him?"[76] "And Cain loved Satan more than God,"[77] and became the father of Satan's lies.[78] Cain was tempted to follow Satan down the road of sin, but Satan could have taken him no further than Cain himself was willing to travel. Being tempted is no excuse for sin and this should serve as a sobering thought to all who would rationalize away their negative behavior as Cain attempted to do.

"My Brother's Flocks"

Was Cain really interested in a few piddling sheep? It stretches one's imagination to think that a person with knowledge enough to make of himself a Son of Perdition would commit murder for a handful of sheep. Joseph Fielding Smith reveals that "Cain slew his brother Abel in order to obtain all the rights of priesthood to descend through his lineage."[79] Cain was not seriously interested in a flock of sheep, but he was concerned about the birthright of the Priesthood. The Priesthood birthright is the right of the oldest worthy male in the family to preside in the Priesthood.[80] In the *Journal of Discourses* it mentions that Cain "might have been the head of this Priesthood, under his father . . . but instead of exercising his birthright on the principles of righteousness, and in accord with the powers of heaven . . ."[81] Cain . . . threw it all away!"[82]

One may ask how it was that Cain had the birthright of the Priesthood seeing that Adam and Eve had many sons and daughters before the birth of Cain. Once again the King James Version is silent on this point, and it is left up to the Inspired Version to answer this question. "And Adam knew his wife, and she bare unto him sons and daughters, and they began to multiply, and to replenish the earth . . . And Adam and Eve blessed the name of God; and they made all things known unto their sons and their daughters. And Satan came among them, saying, I am also a son of God, and he commanded them saying, Believe it not; and they loved Satan more than God. And men began from that time forth to be carnal, sensual and devilish."[83]

In order for Cain to receive the birthright all the previous sons of Adam would have had to have been unworthy and apparently this was the case for when Eve gave birth to Cain she said, "I have gotten a man from the Lord; wherefore he may not reject his words."[84] The inference is that the other sons had rejected the Lord and were thereby not eligible for the Priesthood birthright. So Cain did have a legitimate claim to the birthright for as God said, "If thou doest well thou shalt be accepted."[85] But

Cain did not do well and was not accepted by the Lord. Therefore, he took his place with the rest of the unworthy sons of Adam in not being entitled to possess the Priesthood birthright. It was not until Abel that a righteous son of Adam was found who could step forward and claim by his worthiness the birthright to the Priesthood.

No, it was not a few sheep that Cain coveted, but the birthright that he had lost. Because of his unrighteousness the birthright had passed from Cain to Abel. This was one reason that Cain killed Abel, hoping in some way to gain control over the birthright blessings. By killing Abel, Cain believed the rights of the Priesthood would become his possession.[86] Ironically, Abel still maintained the birthright over Cain. Though he was killed and left without offspring, Abel looked forward to the time when he would be resurrected, exalted, and allowed to utilize his birthright in the Priesthood. For, as the Prophet Joseph proclaimed, Abel is ". . . holding still the keys of his dispensation."[87]

"I Was Wroth"

The offerings that Cain and Abel made to the Lord were symbolic of the faith and worthiness of each. "And the Lord had respect unto Abel and to his offering, but unto Cain, and to his offering, he had not respect . . . and Cain was very wroth, and his countenance fell[88] . . . And Cain went into the field, and Cain talked with Abel, his brother. And it came to pass that while they were in the field, Cain rose up against Abel, his brother, and slew him."[89]

In William Smith's *A Dictionary of the Bible*, it is mentioned that Cain slew Abel "in a fit of jealousy, roused by the rejection of his own sacrifice and the acceptance of Abel's. . . ."[90] As previously mentioned the murder of Abel was not a crime of passion as the above cited dictionary of the Bible would have one believe. The murder was planned and committed in cold blood. The motive for murder involved more than a "fit of jealousy," which explanation most Bible scholars accept. Cain was wroth but it was not anger that caused him to commit murder. As has been explained, Cain killed Abel for the sake of a covenant with Satan and hoped in some way to gain control of the lost birthright.

Why Did Cain Want the Birthright?

It is entirely possible that Cain's motive for killing Abel was more diabolical than simply trying to obtain the birthright itself. There are those who believe that Abel was murdered "not so much with the expectancy of obtaining his brother's worldly possessions, but to cut off [Abel] without posterity. . . ."[91] By holding the birthright to the Priesthood, Abel would have had the privilege of having the Savior come through his lineage. Cain was certainly aware of this blessing. Because he was Perdition and the Father of wickedness Cain attempted to frustrate the plan of God. As Joseph Smith has said, once a man becomes a Son of Perdition he seeks to destroy the kingdom of God and becomes an enemy to Jesus Christ; he will "make open war," seeking always to destroy the plan of salvation.[92]

Not only did Cain want to stop Abel from having children and passing on this birthright of the Priesthood but he also wanted to destroy the birthright itself. Since Cain was Perdition and an enemy to God it was very possible that he hoped the killing of Abel would prevent the Redeemer from coming to earth and making His atoning sacrifice. Had this plan been successful, all would have been subject to Satan without a hope of resurrection or forgiveness of sin. The importance of the Atonement and the fact that without it all who come to earth would be subject to Satan is mentioned in the Book of Mormon:

> Wherefore, it must needs be an infinite atonement—save it should be an infinite atonement this corruption could not put on incorruption. Wherefore, the first judgment which came upon man must needs have remained to an endless duration. And if so, this flesh must have laid down to rot and to crumble to its mother earth, to rise no more.
>
> O the wisdom of God, his mercy and grace! For behold,

if the flesh should rise no more our spirits must become subject to that angel who fell from before the presence of the Eternal God, and became the devil, to rise no more.

And our spirits must have become like unto him, and we become devils, angels to a devil, to be shut out from the presence of our God, and to remain with the father of lies, in misery, like unto himself; yea, to that being who beguiled our first parents, who transformeth himself nigh unto an angel of light, and stirreth up the children of men unto secret combinations of murder and all manner of secret works of darkness.

O how great the goodness of our God, who prepareth a way for our escape from the grasp of this awful monster; yea, that monster, death and hell, which I call the death of the body, and also the death of the spirit.

And because of the way of deliverance of our God, the Holy One of Israel, this death, of which I have spoken, which is the temporal, shall deliver up its dead; which death is the grave.[93]

Without the Atonement all who come to this earth would not only become subject to Satan, but to Cain who will rule over Satan in the eternities.

In his attempt to frustrate the plan of God, Cain, either out of ignorance or misconception, overlooked the possibility of the birthright passing to another son of Adam who was yet unborn. History records that Cain's plan was foiled when Seth received the birthright of the Priesthood.[94]

THE SEED OF CAIN PRESERVED
THROUGH THE FLOOD

BEFORE EMBARKING ON THE QUESTION OF CAIN'S DEscendants today, it becomes necessary to demonstrate that at least one of the children of Cain survived the universal flood. The connection is made when Ham a son of Noah, married Egyptus, a descendant of Cain.[95]

We see that the wife of Ham was named *Egyptus*, which name signifies "that which is forbidden." We know it was the custom in those early times to give to children names conveying a definite meaning based upon some striking event connected with birth or early life, or to point out or fix attention on some peculiarity of character or habit which they may have formed. Frequently, in later life, names were changed because some outstanding event in, or, characteristic of the life of the individual was discovered . . . So it appears very probably that Egyptus was so named because she partook of the curse of her fathers. Moreover, this thought is strengthened in the statement that *from Ham* sprang the race which preserved the curse in the land. The implication seems to be very strong that this curse preserved through the seed of Ham was a curse which came from the other side of the flood. Elder B. H. Roberts several years ago discussed this question as follows:

> Now, why is it that the seed of Ham was cursed as pertaining to the Priesthood? Why is it that his seed 'could not have right to the Priesthood?' Ham's wife was named 'Egyptus, which is forbidden: . . . and thus from Ham sprang the race which preserved the curse in the land.' Was she a descendant of Cain, who was cursed for murdering his brother? And was it by Ham marrying her, and she being saved from the flood in the ark, that 'the race which preserved the curse in the land' was perpetuated? If so, then I believe that race is the one through which it is ordained those spirits that were not valiant in the great rebellion in heaven should come; who rendered themselves unworthy of the Priesthood and its powers, and hence it is withheld from them to this day. Contributor 6:279.[96]

Bruce R. McConkie has acknowledged that "through Ham (a name meaning black) 'the blood of the Canaanites was preserved' through the flood, he having married Egyptus a descendant of Cain. (Abra. 1:20.27.) Negroes are thus descendants of Ham, who himself also was cursed, apparently for marrying into the forbidden lineage. 'Cursed be Canaan; a servant of servants shall he be unto his brethren' (Gen. 9:25), said Noah of Ham's descendants. These descendants cannot hold the Priesthood."[97]

The similarity between the names Egyptus and Egypt is more than a coincidence. Egyptus, the daughter of

Ham, was the progenitor of the original Egyptian people. It should be noted that not only was the mark of Cain preserved through the flood, i.e. a black skin, but the curse of not having the Priesthood as well. The Pearl of Great Price relates the following story. (Abraham 1:21-27):

> 21. Now this king of Egypt was a descendant from the loins of Ham, and was a partaker of the blood of the Canaanites by birth.
>
> 22. From this descent sprang all the Egyptians, and thus the blood of the Canaanites was preserved in the land.
>
> 23. The land of Egypt being first discovered by a woman, who was the daughter of Ham, and the daughter of Egyptus, which in the Chaldean signifies Egypt, which signifies that which is forbidden.
>
> 24. When this woman discovered the land it was under water, who afterward settled her sons in it; and thus, from Ham, sprang that race which preserved the curse in the land.
>
> 25. Now the first government of Egypt was established by Pharaoh, the eldest son of Egyptus, the daughter of Ham, and it was after the manner of the government of Ham, which was patriarchal.
>
> 26. Pharaoh, being a righteous man, established his kingdom and judged his people wisely and justly all his days, seeking earnestly to imitate that order established by the fathers in the first generations, in the days of the first patriarchal reign, even in the reign of Adam, and also of Noah, his father, who blessed him with the blessings of the earth, and with the blessings of wisdom, but cursed him as pertaining to the Priesthood.
>
> 27. Now, Pharaoh . . . [was] of that lineage by which he could not have the right of Priesthood. . . .

So were all the sons and daughters of Ham of that lineage which could not have the right to the Priesthood. Melvin R. Brooks states that Ham "married a Negress, Egyptus, and by this marriage the seed of Cain was perpetuated through and after the flood . . . Ham was the father of four sons: Cush, Mizraim, Phut, and Canaan."[98] His daughter Egyptus carried the same name as his wife and has already been mentioned as the mother of the first

Pharaoh.[99] Modern Negroes can be said to have come from these children of Ham.[100]

The meaning of the names of Ham, his wife, sons, and other descendants indicate a relationship to colored races:

Ham—means "hot," "black."

Egyptus—"that which is forbidden."

Cush—Ethiopia (Ethiopia means "swarthy faced.") . . . dark-skineed race, occupying Eastern Africa, South of Egypt, and Arabia.

Mizraim—Egypt . . . occupied that area in lower Egypt. Mizraim is Hebrew and signifies "Egypt."

Phut or Put—Libyan . . . The Septuagint translates this word as Lybian. From Lybia the Egyptians imported slaves. The inhabitants of Lybia include a goodly portion of Negroes.

Canaan—humiliated . . . He and his people probably settled in Canaan or Palestine. We learn from the Writings of Abraham that these people were black. . . .[101]

FOOTNOTES

[11]*The Holy Bible,* King James Version (London: Collin's Clear Type Press, 1959), Gen. 4:1-17.

[12]*Inspired Version: The Holy Scriptures,* Joseph Smith, Junior (Independence Missouri: Herald Publishing House, 1964), Gen. 5:4-27.

[13]Gen. 4:15; Ezekiel 9:4, King James.

[14]*The Oxford Annotated Bible* (revised standard edition; New York: Oxford University Press, 1962), p. 6.

[15]Louis F. Hartman, C.S.S.R., *Encyclopedic Dictionary of the Bible* (New York: McGraw-Hill, 1963), p. 298.

[16]*Cain and Abel,* Cathedral Film Strip, Old Testament, series one. *The Bible,* 20th Century-Fox.

[17]Robert Young, *Analytical Concordance to the Bible* (twentieth American edition; New York: Funk and Wagnalls Co.), p. 887.

[18]Rt. Rev. S. Fallows, *The Popular and Critical Bible Encyclopedia* (Chicago: The Howard Severance Co., 1905), I:332.

[19]Rev. J. W. Lee, D. D., *New Self-interpreting Bible Library* (Chicago: The Bible Education Society, 1922), I:219.

[20]James Hastings, D. D., *Dictionary of the Bible* (fifth edition; Edinburgh: T and T Clark, 1903), I:3999.

[21]James Strong, "Hebrew and Chaldee Dictionary," *Exhaustive Concordance of the Bible* (New York: Eaton and Mains, 1890), p. 10.

[22]Brigham Young, *Journal of Discourses*, 7:290.

[23]Moses 7:22, *Pearl of Great Price*.

[24]Matthew F. Cowley, *Wilford Woodruff* (Salt Lake City, Utah: Bookcraft, 1964), p. 351, citing Brigham Young's address to the Utah legislature.

[25]Gen. 4:14, King James.

[26]Gen. 4:15, King James.

[27]Rev. J. R. Dummelow, *A Commentary on the Holy Bible* (New York: MacMillian Co, 1949), p. 12.

[28]Hartman, *loc. cit.*

[29]*The Oxford Annotated Bible, loc. cit.*

[30]Fallows, *loc. cit.*

[31]Hastings, *loc. cit.*

[32]Fallows, *op. cit.*, p. 481.

[33]Robert Young, *op. cit.*, p. 216.

[34]Gen. 4:11-12, King James.

[35]Gen. 4:16-17, King James.

[36]Gen. 4:13, King James.

[37]Holy Bible, King James Version, *op. cit.*, p. 4, column reference 9.

[38]*Doctrine and Covenants* 132:27.

[39]Joseph Fielding Smith (comp.), *Teachings of the Prophet Joseph Smith* (Salt Lake City, Utah: Deseret Book Company, 1964), p. 358.

[40]Gen. 4:5-12, *Inspired Version*.

[41]*Doctrine and Covenants*, sec. 22.

[42]Bruce R. McConkie, *Mormon Doctrine* (Salt Lake City, Utah: (Bookcraft, 1958), p. 535.

[43]Moses 5:18, *Pearl of Great Price*.

[44]Moses 5:24, *Pearl of Great Price*.

[45]Ether 8:15, *The Book of Mormon*.

[46]Joseph Fielding Smith, *The Way to Perfection, op. cit.*, p. 98.

[47]*Doctrine and Covenants* 76:44-46.

[48]Gen. 4:15, King James.

[49]Gen. 9:6, King James.

[50]Cowley, *Wilford Woodruff, op. cit.*, p. 351.

[51]Gen. 4:7, King James.

[52]See page   of this book for further explanation of the non-Priesthood line coming through Cain's lineage.

[53]Gen. 4:3, King James.

[54]George A. Buttrick, *The Interpreter's Bible* (New York: Abingdon-Cokesbury Press, 1952), I:58.

[55]Charles W. Penrose, *Journal of Discourses*, 25:47-48.

[56]*Teachings of the Prophet Joseph Smith, op. cit.*, p. 169.

[57]I Sam. 13:13, King James.

[58]Gen. 4:7, King James.

[59]Moses 5:5, *Pearl of Great Price*.

[60]Deut. 26:2-12, King James.

[61]Moses 5:7, *Pearl of Great Price*.

[62]James R. Clark, Ed.D. (comp.), *Messages of the First Presidency, 1833-1964*, (Salt Lake City, Utah: Bookcraft, 1965), I:35-36.

[63]Moses 5:18-19, *Pearl of Great Price.*

[64]Gen. 5:23, *Inspired Version.*

[65]*Ibid.*

[66]*Ibid.*

[67]Gen. 5:15, *Inspired Version.*

[68]Gen. 5:9-10, *Inspired Version.*

[69]Gen. 4:7, King James.

[70]McConkie, *Mormon Doctrine, op. cit.,* p. 102.

[71]Bruce R. McConkie (comp.), *Doctrines of Salvation: Sermons and Writings of Joseph Fielding Smith* (Salt Lake City, Utah: Bookcraft, 1955), II:279.

[72]Hel. 6:25-27, *The Book of Mormon.*

[73]Ether 8:16, *The Book of Mormon.*

[74]Gen. 5:16, *Inspired Version.*

[75]Gen. 4:12, *Inspired Version.*

[76]Gen. 5:4, *Inspired Version.*

[77]Gen. 5:6, *Inspired Version.*

[78]Gen. 5:9, *Inspired Version.*

[79]Joseph Fielding Smith, *Answers to Gospel Questions, op. cit.,* 2:188.

[80]McConkie, *Mormon Doctrine, op. cit.,* p. 82-83.

[81]Erastus Snow, *Journal of Discourses,* 21:370.

[82]Joseph Fielding Smith, *The Way to Perfection, op. cit.,* p. 97.

[83]Gen. 4:2, 12, 13, *Inspired Version.*

[84]Gen. 5:4, *Inspired Version.*

[85]Gen. 5:9, *Inspired Version.*

[86]Joseph Fielding Smith, *Answers to Gospel Questions, op. cit.,* 2:188.

[87]*Teachings of the Prophet Joseph Smith, op. cit.,* p. 169.

[88]Gen. 4:5, King James.

[89]Gen. 4:8, King James.

[90]William Smith, *A Dictionary of the Bible,* p. 100.

[91]Joseph Fielding Smith, *The Way to Perfection, op. cit.,* p. 101.

[92]*Teachings of the Prophet Joseph Smith, op. cit.,* p. 358.

[93]II Nephi 9:7-11, *The Book of Mormon.*

[94]Erastus Snow, *Journal of Discourses,* 21:370-371; Gen. 4:25, King James.

[95]Abraham 1:20-27.

[96]Joseph Fielding Smith, *The Way to Perfection, op. cit.,* pp. 104-105.

[97]McConkie, *Mormon Doctrine, op. cit.,* p. 314.

[98]Melvin R. Brooks, *LDS Reference Encyclopedia* (Salt Lake City, Utah: Bookcraft, 1960), p. 167.

[99]Abraham 1:25, *Pearl of Great Price.*

[100]Brooks, *loc. cit.*

[101]*Ibid.*

V

WHAT ABOUT THE NEGRO
AND THE PRIESTHOOD?

A T VARIOUS TIMES IN THE STORY OF CAIN IT HAS BEEN pointed out that his posterity would not be entitled to the Priesthood. This is true with the very important qualification of time. There are those both in and out of the Church who believe that the Negroes will never hold the Priesthood. According to Brigham Young, in a speech on this topic, "They [Negroes]will then come up and possess the Priesthood, and receive all the blessings which we are entitled to."[102]

It is now necessary that a close examination be made of why the Negroes are not allowed to hold that Priesthood at this time. In doing so, it will be shown that the reasons for withholding the Priesthood from the Negroes during mortality have nothing whatsoever to do with discrimination, prejudice, or racial bias. When all the principles touching this matter are understood it will be evident that God is truly just and His Church "is not a respecter of persons."[103]

There are three basic points that need to be taken into consideration if one is to understand the question of the Negro and the Priesthood. These are: (1) What is the Priesthood? (2) Why can't the Negroes hold the Priesthood now? (3) When will the Negroes be allowed to possess the Priesthood?

WHAT IS THE PRIESTHOOD?

A NON-MORMON MAY PROPERLY INQUIRE, "WHAT IS THE Priesthood?" Priesthood is divine authority which is conferred upon men that they may officiate in the ordi-

nances of the Gospel. . . . Priesthood is a part of God's
own power which he bestows upon his chosen servants that
they may act in his name in proclaiming the gospel and
officiating in all the ordinances thereof."[104] "Priesthood is
authority and power given by God to man to act in God's
name."[105] "The Holy Priesthood is the channel through
which God communicates and deals with man upon the
earth."[106]

The Priesthood then is the right to act in God's name
and have those acts recognized by God. In other words,
it is that power that Christ gave Peter when He said,
"And I will give unto thee the keys of the kingdom of
heaven: and whatsoever thou shalt bind on earth shall be
bound in heaven: and whatsoever thou shalt loose on
on earth shall be loosed in heaven."[107] A bearer of the
proper Priesthood can baptize an individual by the authority of that Priesthood and God will recognize that baptism
as valid in the life to come. The Priesthood is the right
to perform with authority the ordinances of the Gospel.

In commenting about the Priesthood, Wilford Woodruff said, ". . . and without this Priesthood, no man, from
the day the world rolled into existence, has any right to
administer in any of the ordinances of His holy house
neither has any man a right to that Priesthood save he be
called of God as was Aaron who, we are informed was
called by revelation."[108] As Paul mentioned to the He-
brews, ". . . and no man taketh this honour unto himself,
but he that is called of God, as was Aaron."[109]

The point has been mentioned that Aaron was called
by a revelation from God through Moses. Accordingly
the Priesthood is also denied to all but those who are in
authority. "All men who assume authority, but who have
not been properly called, will have to answer for their
acts in the day of judgment. Nothing that they perform
in the name of the Lord is valid, for it lacks the stamp of
divine authority. To deceive and lead others to believe
that unauthorized acts are valid when performed in the
name of the Lord is a grievous sin in the sight of God."[110]

Mormons believe there is only one true Priesthood on the earth today. This Priesthood, after having been taken from the earth,[111] was restored to Joseph Smith in 1829, by heavenly messengers under the direction of Jesus Christ.[112] The keys of the Priesthood have been passed down from Joseph to the present prophet by divine revelation and by the laying on of hands by those who are in authority. *It is this authority to act in the name of God in performing ordinances of the Gospel that is at present denied the Negroes.*

WHY CAN'T THE NEGROES HOLD
THE PRIESTHOOD NOW?

THERE ARE TWO MAJOR REASONS WHY THE NEGROES are not allowed to hold the Priesthood at present. The first reason deals with the concept of a proper time; the second has to do with the LDS belief in a pre-mortal life.

A Proper Time to Hold the Priesthood

The question is not one of holding or not holding the Priesthood. The question is one of *time!* Many ask, "Why can't the Negroes have the Priesthood now?" The answer is amazingly simple. It is not yet time. The concept of proper time is not one to be decided by popular vote or majority rule but by commandment from God. The people of Israel did not enter the promised land as soon as they arrived at the borders of their inheritance. They were commanded that they wander for forty years in the wilderness because the time was not yet right, the people were not yet ready.[113]

Some have difficulty accepting the idea of God not being a respecter of persons with the idea that at present the Negroes are not allowed to hold the Priesthood. To those people that find difficulty in accepting this, we present the case of Jesus not being sent to the Gentiles during His earthly ministry but only to the Jews. Shortly after the Lord gave His Priesthood to the original twelve apostles He gave them a commandment, "Go not into the way of the Gentile, and into any city of the Samaritans enter ye not."[114]   Was this flagrant discrimination, or could it be that in the wisdom of the Lord the time was not yet that the Gospel was to be carried to the Gentiles? The Lord further instructed His disciples to "go rather to the lost sheep of the house of Israel [Jews]."[115]   When once a woman of Canaan came out to seek the Savior's help in curing her daughter who was vexed with an evil spirit, the Lord did not even speak to her but rather turned to His disciples and explained, "I am not sent but unto the lost sheep of the house of Israel."[116]   It was not until the advent of Paul and his special call that the Gospel message of Christ was carried to the gentile world.

The Savior knew that "to every thing there is a season, and a time to every purpose under the heaven:"[117]

> A time to be born, and a time to die; a time to plant, and a time to pluck up that which is planted;
> A time to kill, and a time to heal; a time to break down, and a time to build up;
> A time to weep, and a time to laugh; a time to mourn, and a time to dance;
> A time to cast away stones, and a time to gather stones together; a time to embrace, and a time to refrain from embracing;
> A time to get, and a time to lose; a time to keep, and a time to cast away;
> A time to rend, and a time to sew; a time to keep silence, and a time to speak;
> A time to love, and a time to hate; a time of war, and a time of peace.[118]

It could very well be added, a time to hold the Priesthood, and a time not to hold the Priesthood.

On one occasion, the Lord knew that if He left Galilee and entered Judea during the Feast of Tabernacles, He would probably be killed. His brethren encouraged Him to go anyway, saying that if He were the Son of God He had nothing to hide; He likewise had nothing to fear. But Jesus sent them ahead to the feast with these words,

"My time is not yet full come. . . ."[119]

Our Lord was fully aware of the necessity of events occurring at the proper time. During the last week of His life the Master sent His disciples into Jerusalem to prepare for the final passover meal with these instructions for a certain man, "The Master saith, My time is at hand. . ."[120] If Christ, the perfect Son of God, had times and bounds set upon His mortal existence, is it not probable that others of the human family would also be subject to times and bounds?

The concept of proper time is a golden thread that is woven throughout the story of the Bible and God's dealings with man. Could it be possible that, "it is not for you to know the times or the seasons, which the Father hath put in his own power"?[121] Is it man's responsibility to "determine the times before appointed, and the bounds of their habitation. . . ."?[122] Is it just possible that mortals "know not the thoughts of the Lord, neither understand . . . His counsel. . . ."?[123] Could it be that if we were to take it upon ourselves to give the Negroes the Priesthood of God, that it would prove to be a curse instead of a blessing at this time, especially when the Lord has said through His prophets that there is a time appointed for them to receive it, but that time is not now? Would anyone in the name of social justice or equality care to challenge the Lord, because God, whose work it is to "bring to pass the immortality and eternal life of man,"[124] does not know what He is doing?

As President David O. McKay has expressed, "Sometime in God's eternal plan, the Negro will be given the right to hold the Priesthood. In the meantime, those of that race who receive the testimony of the Restored Gospel may have their family ties protected and other blessings made secure, for in the justice and mercy of the Lord they will possess all the blessings to which they are entitled in the eternal plan of salvation and exaltation."[125]

A Pre-mortal Life

In order to understand why the Negroes are not

allowed to have the Priesthood at this time, it is essential
that the doctrine of the Latter-day Saints concerning a
pre-mortal life be explained. It is this doctrine more than
any other that will aid the non-Mormon in understanding
the LDS position about the Negro.

By pre-mortal life is meant a previous existence as
individuals before coming to this earth.[126] Specifically,
the doctrine refers to a pre-existence in another sphere
with God, as His sons and daughters in His heavenly home.
Mormons believe that every man, woman, and child, black
and white alike, is a literal spirit son or daughter of
heavenly parents. As President Heber J. Grant stated,
"The doctrine of pre-existence pours a wonderful flood of
light upon the otherwise mysterious problem of man's
origin. It shows that man, as a spirit was begotten and
born of heavenly parents and reared to maturity in the
eternal mansions of the Father prior to coming upon the
earth in a temporal body to undergo an experience in
mortality."[127]

There are those who scoff at the idea of a pre-mortal
life. Many of these same people, however, have full
confidence in an after-life and look forward to dwelling
in Heaven, Shangri-La, or Nirvana. If the spirit of man
is eternal, does it seem so unusual that he should have
a pre-existence to this earth life as well as a post-existence?
Is it consistent to say that the spirit of man is eternal,
immortal, and everlasting on the one hand, and on the
other, say that man's spirit begins at birth into mortality?

The belief in pre-mortal life is not only logical, it is
a doctrine that is supported by Biblical scriptures. Did
not the Savior ask the Father to glorify Him with the
glory He had before the world was; thus, inferring a pre-
mortal existence of Christ?[128] Was not pre-existent life
implied when God spoke to Job saying, "Where wast thou
when I laid the foundations of the earth? declare, if thou
hast understanding. . . . When the morning stars sang
together, and all the sons of God shouted for joy [where
wast thou]"?[129] Are we not told that Jeremiah was appointed to a mission in this life before birth?[130]

Paul makes the assertion that "We have had fathers of our flesh which corrected us and we gave them reverence; shall we not much rather be in subjection to the Father of spirits, and live?"[131] As Paul inferred, we have earthly parents and heavenly parents. This would imply that we have two births, i.e., a spiritual birth and a mortal birth. Before our spirits joined with our bodies to partake of mortal life, we were born as spirits in another sphere. It is the LDS belief that God, our Heavenly Father, is our literal spirit parent. We are all members of the same Celestial family, for as Paul said, ". . . [God] hath made of one blood all nations of men for to dwell on all the face of the earth, . . ."[132] It is for this reason that every person on earth is considered a brother or sister regardless of race.

Our spirits dwelt with our Father in Heaven for a great while prior to our coming to this earth. Joseph F. Smith explains,

> Our spirits existed before they came to this world. They were in the councils of the heavens before the foundations of the earth were laid. We were there; we were interested, and we took part in this great preparation. We were unquestionably present in those councils, . . . when Satan offered himself as a savior of the world, if he could but receive the honor and the glory of the Father for doing it. But Jesus said, "Father, Thy will be done, and the glory be Thine forever." Wherefore because Satan rebelled against God, and sought to destroy the agency [freedom] of man, the Father rejected him and he was cast out, but Jesus was accepted. (Rev. 12:7-9.) We were, no doubt, there and took part in all those scenes; we were vitally concerned in the carrying out of these great plans and purposes; we understood them, and it was for our sakes they were decreed and are to be consummated. These spirits have been coming to this earth to take upon them tabernacles, that they might become like unto Jesus Christ—being "formed in His likeness and image," from the morn of creation until now, and will continue until the winding-up scene, until the spirits who were destined to come to this world shall have come and accomplished their mission in the flesh.[133]

The pre-existence was only a part of the over-all plan that God had designed for the salvation of His children. The pre-earth life was a time of preparation and growth. Earth life was to be a time of test and trials.[134] The post-earth period was to be a time of rewards and punishments. Brigham Young commented about this plan saying,

> It is the wish of our Heavenly Father to bring all His children back into His presence. The spirits of all the human family dwelt with Him before they took tabernacles of flesh and became subject to the fall and to sin. He is their spiritual Father and has sent them here to be clothed with flesh and to be subject, with their tabernacles, to the ills that afflict fallen humanity. When they have proved themselves faithful in all things, and worthy before Him, they can then have the privilege of returning again to His presence, with their bodies, to dwell in the abodes of the blessed.[135]

The thought of man dwelling with God prior to coming to this earth is for some incomprehensible. The point is, however, that Mormons do believe it.

Pre-existent Free Agency

It is a precept of Mormonism that in the pre-existent state men and women had their freedom of choice, often called free agency. Joseph Fielding Smith mentions, "God gave His children their free agency even in the spirit world, by which the individual spirits had the privilege, just as men here, of choosing the good and rejecting the evil, or partaking of the evil to suffer the consequences of their sins."[136] Not only did man live with God in the pre-mortal life, but he also had his free agency.

It will be noted that free agency is not complete license to do whatsoever one will without regard for the consequences of one's acts. Free agency is but one side of a two-edged sword. The other side is responsibility for one's own behavior. In the pre-existence each utilized his freedom of choice fully cognizant that he would be held accountable for the mis-use of it. Each realized that the responsibility for his acts would rest upon his own shoulders. "God gave His children their free agency even in the spirit world, by which the individual spirits had the privilege, just as men here, of choosing the good and rejecting the evil, or partaking of the evil to suffer the consequences of their sins. Because of this, some even there were more faithful than others in keeping the commandments of the Lord."[137]

Abraham was aware of the differences that existed between individuals in the pre-existence when he said, "Now the Lord had shown unto me, Abraham, the intelligences that were organized before the world was; and among all these there were many of the noble and great ones."[138] From this statement it is inferred that there were some who were not noble or great in the pre-existence. Why were they not noble or great? They chose not to be by the use of their pre-mortal free agency which was their perfect right.

Pre-existent Judgment

Before coming to earth, each child of our Heavenly Father was judged on an individual basis according to how he used his free agency. The "law of the harvest," which is an eternal principle, was very much in effect in the pre-existence. Whatsoever ye sow, that also shall ye reap.[139] The great justice of God begins to unfold as one realizes that each person receives opportunities in this world according to his own pre-mortal behavior. This truth so long overlooked by the world is a matter of simple justice. Is it not true that one's future existence and happiness depend to a great extent on what he does now? Are we not told in the scriptures that each man will be assigned an eternal and everlasting weight of glory in God's heaven according to his works upon this earth?

> And I saw the dead, small and great, stand before God; and the books were opened: and another book was opened, which is the book of life: and the dead were judged out of those things which were written in ths books, according to their works.
>
> And the sea gave up the dead which were in it; and death and hell delivered up the dead which were in them:

AND THEY WERE JUDGED EVERY MAN ACCORDING
TO THEIR WORKS.[140]

Just as we are going to be judged according to our
works in this life, we were judged according to our works
in the pre-mortal life. "The labors that we performed in
the sphere that we left before we came here have had a
certain effect upon our lives here, and to a certain extent
they govern and control the lives that we lead here, just
the same as the labors that we do here will control and
govern our lives when we pass from this stage of existence."[41]

We have learned through the word of the Lord to
Abraham that spirits in the pre-existence were graded.
Some were cast out of heaven altogether, some sent to
the earth with certain restrictions placed upon them, and
some were sent to this earth as a chosen people.[142] It
is written that Satan and one-third of the host of heaven
were cast out completely[143] and allowed to come to this
earth only as spirits, being forbidden to partake of mortal
bodies. ". . . There were other spirits there who were not
faithful in the keeping of this first estate. Yet they have
not sinned away their right to receive bodies and come to
earth and receive the resurrection."[144] These come to
earth with certain limitations.

It is the Mormon belief that in our pre-mortal state
there were a large number of individuals who, due to
some act or behavior of *their own* in the pre-existence,
forfeited the right to hold the Priesthood during their mortal lives, but would be allowed to possess the Priesthood
in the due time of the Lord.[145] It is not specifically known
what these individuals did or did not do in the pre-existence to be denied the Priesthood. It is only known that
whatever it was, it was a matter of individual responsibility and choice.[146] We are told by our prophets, both
ancient and modern, that these individuals would all be
assigned to the same race and that they were all to come
through a lineage which would be forbidden the Priesthood during mortality. "Therefore the Lord prepared a

way through the lineage of Cain for these spirits to come to the earth, but under the restriction of priesthood."[147] That group is known today as the Negroid race.

Negroes, we see, "were not denied the privilege of receiving the second estate [mortality] but were permitted to come to the earthlife with some restrictions placed upon them. That the Negro race, for instance, had been placed under restrictions because of their attitude in the world of spirits, few will doubt. It cannot be looked upon as just that they should be deprived of the power of the Priesthood without it being a punishment for some act, or acts, performed before they were born."[148] The Negro is thus denied the Priesthood because of his own behavior in the pre-existence. As Joseph Fielding Smith tells us,

> There is a reason why one man is born black with other disadvantages, while another is born white with great advantages. The reason is that we once had an estate before we came here, and were obedient, more or less, to the laws that were given us there. Those who were faithful in all things there received greater blessings here and those who were not so faithful received less . . . Every man had his agency there, and men received rewards here based upon their actions there, just as they will receive rewards hereafter for deeds done in the body. The Negro, evidently is receiving the reward he merits."[149]

There have been different groups sent to the earth with other restrictions. It is not a matter of the Lord singling out one race and discriminating against them. The Lord does not discriminate at all. President McKay explained,

> By the operation of some unwritten eternal law with which man is yet unfamiliar, spirits come through parentages for which they are worthy—some as Bushmen of Australia, some as Solomon Islanders, some as Americans, as Europeans, as Asiatics, etc., etc., with all the varying degrees of mentality and spirituality manifest in parents of the different races that inhabit the earth.

> Of this we may be sure, each was satisfied and happy to come through the lineage to which he or she was attracted and for which, and only which, he or she was prepared."[150]

The race into which one is born is not an arbitrary assignment but the result of one's works and worthiness in the pre-existence. Every person is entitled to the blessings which deal specifically with his race. Groups with similar judgments and blessings of worthiness were sent to earth in the same race. When one comes to the realization that God has placed each person on earth according to his abilities and talents, it gives one a deep sense of respect for a Father in Heaven who judges all of His children fairly and impartially. Referring to the circumstances into which people are born, Bruce R. McConkie has written, "The race and nation in which men are born in this world is a direct result of their pre-existent life. All the spirit host of heaven deemed worthy to receive bodies were fore-ordained to pass through this earthly probation in the particular race and nation suited to their needs, circumstances, and talents."[151]

Not Suffering For Cain's Transgression

The evidence seems to be clear that Cain's descendants have a skin of black and are prevented from holding the Priesthood because of their own pre-existent behavior. As stated in our second Article of Faith, "We believe that men will be punished for their own sins, and not for Adam's transgression."[152] Holding to this same reasoning, the Negroes are not being restricted for Cain's sins but for their own acts in the pre-existence.

Many people become confused and frustrated in their attempt to understand the relationship between Cain and his descendants. However, when one understands the doctrine of a pre-existent life and judgement, the issue is readily comprehended. Cain's curse and the curse that came upon his descendants are the result of two totally different set of circumstances. Cain's malediction was a result of his behavior during his mortal probation. He was cursed because of his rejection of God and his love of Satan. On the other hand, the Negroes are restricted as to the Priesthood because of their behavior in the pre-mortal life. The only real relationship between Cain and the Negroes is that they were chosen to come through Cain's lineage. Negroes are not Sons of Perdition as Cain was, but are beloved children of a just God.

WHEN WILL THE NEGROES RECEIVE THE PRIESTHOOD?

B RIGHAM YOUNG REVEALED THAT THE NEGROES WILL NOT receive the Priesthood until a great while after the second advent of Jesus Christ, whose coming will usher in a millennium of peace.[153]

Revelation?

In view of what President Young and others have said, it would be foolish indeed to give anyone the false idea that a new revelation is immediately forthcoming on the issue of the Negroes receiving the Priesthood. If the prophet of God were to receive a revelation tomorrow giving the Negroes the Priesthood it would certainly be accepted regardless of what Brigham Young or any previous prophet has said. This is because the words of the living oracles relate more specifically to the era in which we live. The fact is, however, that our present prophets are in complete agreement with Brigham Young and other past leaders on the question of the Negro and the Priesthood. President McKay was asked by a news reporter at the dedication of the Oakland Temple, "When will the Negroes receive the Priesthood?" He responded to the question over a national television network saying, "Not in my lifetime, young man, nor yours."[154]

Mormons view a prophet as God's literal mouthpiece on earth. When a prophet speaks as a prophet, it carries the same force as one of the Ten Commandments. This is because of the Mormon belief in continuous revelation. The faithful Latter-day Saint accepts the prophet's words as God's will. Prophets do not inspire God; God inspires prophets.

Social pressure and even government sanctions cannot be expected to bring forth a new revelation. This point is mentioned because there are groups in the Church, as well as out, who feel that pressure on the Prophet will cause a revelation to come forth. It would be wise to emphasize that all the social pressure in the world will not change what the Lord has decreed to be. Let those who would pressume to pressure the Prophet be reminded that it is God that inspires prophets, not social pressure. To this same group, the words of Paul should serve as a caution. "Beware lest any man spoil you through philosophy and vain deceit, after the tradition of men, after the rudiments of the world, and not after Christ."[155]

The Prophet Joseph explained that every member of the Church has the privilege of receiving revelation pertaining to his particular calling and duty in the Church. No one has the right, however, of receiving revelation for an office or calling held by another. Bishops do not receive revelation for stake presidents; deacons do not receive revelation for apostles. No one but the president of the Church may receive a revelation for the Church. "Revelations of the mind and will of God to the Church are to come through the presidency. This is the order of heaven . . ."[156] The first presidency of the Church on August 17, 1951, made an official statement concerning a change in the doctrine of the Negro and the Priesthood. "It is not a matter of . . . policy but of direct commandment from the Lord."[157]

We must have faith in a just God and rely on what the prophets have given us. When the proper time arrives, the Negroes will be given the Priesthood just as the Gentiles were taught the Gospel in the due time of the Lord. It is not the responsibility nor the stewardship of any person on earth to dictate to the Lord or the Lord's servants when a revelation should be given. When the time comes for a revelation "surely the Lord God will do nothing, but He revealeth His secret unto His servants the prophets."[158]

Two Stipulations Before the Priesthood Can be Given

The prophets have declared that there are at least two major stipulations that have to be met before the Negroes will be allowed to possess the Priesthood. The first requirement relates to time. The Negroes will not be allowed to hold the Priesthood during mortality, in fact, not until after the resurrection of all of Adam's children. The other stipulation requires that Abel's seed receive the first opportunity of having the Priesthood.

Adam's Children Resurrected

Brigham Young disclosed in a speech delivered in the Salt Lake tabernacle on December 3, 1854, that the Negroes will not have the privilege of receiving the Priesthood until ". . . all the other children of Adam have had the privilege of receiving the Priesthood, and of coming into the kingdom of God, and of being redeemed from the four quarters of the earth, and have received their resurrection from the dead, then it will be time enough to remove the curse from Cain and his posterity."[159] Some twelve years later in 1866, Brigham Young again commented on the Negro and the Priesthood. In this speech he is quoted as saying, "They [Negroes] will go down to death. And when all the rest of the children [of Adam] have received their blessings in the Holy Priesthood, then that curse will be removed from the seed of Cain, and they will come up and possess the priesthood and receive all the blessings we now are entitled to."[160]

It is clearly stated in the above quotes that the Negroes must first pass through mortality before they may possess the Priesthood ("they will go down to death"). Reference is also made to the condition that the Negroes will have to wait until after the resurrection of all of Adam's children before receiving the Priesthood. It might be well to examine for a moment the question of the resurrection. Bruce R. McConkie has said,

> Nothing is more absolutely universal than the resurrection. Every living being will be resurrected. "As in Adam all die, even so in Christ shall all be made alive." (I. Cor.

15:22). Two great resurrections await the inhabitants of
the earth: one is the first resurrection, . . . the resurrection
of the just; the other is the second resurrection, . . . the
resurrection of the unjust. (John 5:28-29; Rev. 20; D&C
76) . . . The first resurrection, for those who have lived
since Christ's resurrection will occur at the time of the
Second Coming. At the end of the millennium, the second
resurrection begins: "And these are the rest of the dead;
and they live not again until the thousand years are ended."
(D&C 88:101).[161]

All of this means that the last of Adam's children will not
be resurrected until the end of the millennium. Therefore,
the Negroes will not receive the Priesthood until after
that time. It would be well to point out that the exact
time for the Negroes to be given the Priesthood after the
millennium is not known. It is only known that this will
not happen until after the thousand years of Christ's reign
on earth.

After Abel's Seed

The second major stipulation that needs to be met before the Negroes can be allowed to possess the Priesthood
is the requirement that Abel's seed receive the opportunity
of holding the Priesthood first. The Prophet Joseph taught
that Negroes could not hold the Priesthood or act in any
of its offices until the seed of Abel received that Priesthood.[162] This seems like a rather unusual requirement
until one understands the nature of this provision. By
killing Abel, "Cain deprived his brother of the privilege of
pursuing his journey through life, and of extending his
kingdom by multiplying upon the earth; and because he
did this, he is the last to share the joys of the kingdom
of God."[163]

It was a great tragedy for Abel to be killed and thereby
prevented from having any offspring. It is written that the
blessings of exaltation consist in "the continuation of the
family unit in eternity"[164] and a "continuation of the
seeds forever and ever."[165] Abel was unrighteously kept
from establishing any family ties or of being the progenitor
of a great nation. The children that were to come to

earth through the lineage of Abel had to be redirected through other lines.[166] Abel was thus denied a tremendous blessing of having millions of spirits descending from him. Until Abel can have seed and until they have an opportunity of receiving the Priesthood, Cain's descendants will not be allowed to have that Priesthood. Wilford Woodruff tells us, ". . . until the seed of Abel shall be redeemed . . . Cain shall not receive the priesthood, until the time of that [seed of Abel's] redemption."[167]

The obvious question is, "When will Abel's seed be redeemed?" It will first of all be necessary that Abel marry, and then be resurrected, and ultimately exalted in the highest degree of the Celestial Kingdom so that he can have a continuation of his seed.[168] It will then be necessary for Abel to create an earth for his spirit children to come to and experience mortality. These children will have to be "redeemed" or resurrected. After the resurrection or redemption of Abel's seed, Cain's descendants, the Negroes, will then be allowed to possess the Priesthood. Joseph Fielding Smith has said that "the Lord decreed that the children of Cain should not have the privilege of bearing the priesthood until ABEL HAD POSTERITY who could have the priesthood and that will have to be in the FAR DISTANT FUTURE. When this is accomplished ON SOME OTHER WORLD, then the restrictions will be removed from the children of Cain who have been true to their 'second' estate."[169] This earth life is considered the "second" estate and those Negroes who prove through their individual righteousness their worth will certainly be blessed by God to possess the Priesthood in that distant future when Abel's seed has been redeemed.

It is vitally important to re-emphasize at this point that Cain's descendants are not being denied the Priesthood because of the sins of Cain. The fact that they are required to wait this great length of time in order to receive the Priesthood is not because of Cain's slaying of Abel, but because of their own individual preparation and worthiness in the pre-existence.

FOOTNOTES

[102]Brigham Young, *Journal of Discourses*, II:272.

[103]Romans 2:11, King James.

[104]Joseph Fielding Smith, *Doctrines of Salvation*, (1956), *op. cit.*, III:80.

[105]Brooks, *L.D.S. Reference Encyclopedia, op. cit.*, p. 393.

[106]Daniel H. Ludlow (ed.), *Latter-day Prophets Speak* (Salt Lake City, Utah: Bookcraft, 1951), p. 183.

[107]Matt. 16:19, King James.

[108]Wilford Woodruff, *Journal of Discourses*, 19:360.

[109]Heb. 5:4, King James.

[110]Joseph Fielding Smith, *Doctrines of Salvation, op. cit.*, III:81.

[111]Amos 8:11-12, Isa. 29:13-14; Acts 20:29-30; Gal. 1:6-9; II Thess. 2:1-11; I Tim. 4:1-3; II Peter 2:1-3. (These scripture indicate an apostasy.)

[112]Joseph Smith 2:1-75, *Pearl of Great Price.*

[113]Num. 32:9-14, King James.

[114]Matt. 10:5, King James.

[115]Matt. 10:6, King James.

[116]Matt. 15:24, King James.

[117]Eccl. 3:1, King James.

[118]Eccl. 3:2-8, King James.

[119]John 7:1-8, King James.

[120]Matt. 26:18, King James.

[121]Acts 1:7, King James.

[122]Acts 17:26, King James.

[123]Micah 4:12, King James.

[124]Moses 1:39, *Pearl of Great Price.*

[125]Berrett, "The Church and the Negroid People," *Mormonism and the Negro, op. cit.*, p. 23.

[126]Joseph Fielding Smith, *Doctrines of Salvation*, (1954), *op. cit.*, I:56.

[127]Ludlow, *Latter-day Prophets Speak, op. cit.*, p. 4.

[128]Heb. 12:9, King James.

[129]Job 38:4, 7, King James.

[130]Jer. 1:4-5, King James.

[131]Heb. 12:9, King James.

[132]Acts 17:26, King James.

[133]Joseph F. Smith, *Journal of Discourses*, 25:57.

[134]Abraham 3:25, *Pearl of Great Price.*

[135]Ludlow, *Latter-day Prophets Speak, op. cit.*, p. 13.

[136]Joseph Fielding Smith, *Doctrines of Salvation, op. cit.*, I:58.

[137]*Ibid.*, pp. 58-59.

[138]Abraham 3:22, *Pearl of Great Price.*

[139]II Cor. 9:6, King James.

[140]Rev. 20:12-13, King James.

[141]Ludlow, *Latter-day Prophets Speak, op. cit.*, p. 7, quote by Heber J. Grant.

[142]Joseph Fielding Smith, *The Way to Perfection, op. cit.,* p. 42.

[143]Rev. 12:7-9.

[144]Joseph Fielding Smith, *Answers to Gospel Questions, op. cit.,* 2:186.

[145]Brigham Young, *Journal of Discourses,* 2:143.

[146]Melvin R. Ballard (comp.), *Melvin J. Ballard—Crusader for Righteousness* (Salt Lake City, Utah: Bookcraft, 1966), p. 218.

[147]Joseph Fielding Smith, *Answers to Gospel Questions, op. cit.,* 2:186.

[148]Joseph Fielding Smith, *The Way to Perfection, op. cit.,* pp. 43-44.

[149]Joseph Fielding Smith, *Doctrines of Salvation, op. cit.,* I:61, 66.

[150]Berrett, "The Church and the Negroid People," *Mormonism and The Negro, op. cit.,* pp. 22-23.

[151]McConkie, *Mormon Doctrine, op. cit.,* p. 554.

[152]"The Articles of Faith," (No. 2), *The Pearl of Great Price,* p. 59.

[153]Brigham Young, *Journal of Discourses,* 2:143.

[154]Dedication of the Oakland Temple, Tuesday, November 17, 1964.

[155]Col. 2:8.

[156]*Teachings of the Prophet Joseph Smith, op. cit.,* p. 111.

[157]Berrett, "The Church and the Negroid People," *Mormonism and the Negro, op. cit.,* p. 16.

[158]Amos 3:7.

[159]Brigham Young, *Journal of Discourses,* 2:143.

[160]Brigham Young, *Journal of Discourses,* 11:272.

[161]McConkie, *Mormon Doctrine, op. cit.,* pp. 573-79.

[162]Milton R. Hunter, *Pearl of Great Price Commentary* (Salt Lake City Utah: Bookcraft, 1951), p. 142.

[163]Brigham Young, *Journal of Discourses,* 2:143.

[164]McConkie, *Mormon Doctrine, op. cit.,* p. 238.

[165]*Doctrine and Covenants* 132:19.

[166]Gen. 4:25.

[167]Cowley, *Wilford Woodruff, op. cit.,* p. 351, citing Brigham Young.

[168]*Doctrine and Covenants* 132:19-21.

[169]Joseph Fielding Smith, *Answers to Gospel Questions, op. cit.,* 2:188.

VI

INTERRACIAL MARRIAGE AND THE NEGRO

BEFORE THE DOCTRINE ON INTERRACIAL MARRIAGE CAN
be understood, it becomes necessary to examine the
concept of a Chosen People. "Blessed is the nation whose
God is the Lord; and the people whom he hath chosen for
his own inheritance."[170] It has already been mentioned
that each one received an assignment to a race, time, and
nation on this earth according to his individual worthiness
and preparation in the pre-existence.

> The race and nation in which men are born in this
> world is a direct result of their pre-existent life. All the
> spirit host of heaven deemed worthy to receive mortal bodies
> were foreordained to pass through this earthly probation in
> the particular race and nation suited to their needs, cir-
> cumstances, and talents. "When the Most High divided to
> the nations their inheritance, when he separated the sons
> of Adam," Moses said with reference to the number of the
> children of Israel." (Deut. 32:8.) Not only Israel, but all
> groups were thus foreknown and their total membership
> designated in the pre-mortal life. Paul spoke similarly when
> he averred that God "hath made of one blood all nations of
> men for to dwell on all the face of the earth, and hath
> determined the times before appointed, and the bounds of
> their habitation." (Acts 17:26).[171]

It becomes obvious that the Chosen People were chosen
before they came into mortality. The scriptures tell that
in the pre-existence there were many noble and great
ones.[172] Of these it is said, "And God saw these souls
that they were good, and he stood in the midst of them,
and he said: These I will make my rulers; for he stood
among those that were spirits and he saw that they were
good; and he said unto me: Abraham, thou art one of
them; thou wast chosen before thou wast born."[173] A
similar statement concerning a person who was chosen before birth was made when the Lord said to Jeremiah,

"Before I formed thee in the belly I knew thee; and before thou camest forth out of the womb I sanctified thee, and I ordained thee a prophet unto the nations."[174] Joseph Smith mentioned that "every man who has a calling to minister to the inhabitants of the world was ordained to that very purpose in the Grand Council of Heaven before this world was . . ."[175] Those who were chosen to be of the Chosen People during mortality were thus selected prior to birth because of their acts in the pre-existence. They were selected because they were "noble and great."

One might ask why it was necessary to have the noble and great ones come to earth and be members of a certain race. The answer is found in a statement by Bruce R. McConkie: ". . . each righteous spirit called to minister in priestly offices has been ordained to come through a particular lineage. Consequently it has become the right of those holding the special inheritance in the Lord's chosen lineage to receive the priesthood, provided they are obedient and faithful."[176] In other words the Chosen are chosen to have the Priesthood and the accompanying blessings if they prove worthy in this life. The blessing of the Priesthood is one of several opportunities that has been given to the Chosen People.

Each race and nation is afforded different opportunities. Those of similar blessings, preparation, and worthiness in the pre-existence were sent to this earth through the race for which they were best prepared.[177] It is for this reason that God warned Israel not to intermarry with those of other races. Intermarriage would bring a polution of the seed with its subsequent loss of blessings. In the case of modern Israel, intermarriage with the Negro means the loss of Priesthood blessings.

The Church is aware that its stand on interracial marriage may not be a popular one. It nevertheless believes that there is a greater tribunal than social opinion and that keeping the commandments of the Lord is more important than pleasing the masses. In a letter from the First Presidency to Dr. Lowery Nelson, one time head of the Dept. of Sociology at B.Y.U., the question of inter-racial marriage was discussed:

> Your ideas, as we understand them, appear to con-template the intermarriage of the Negro and White races, a concept which has heretofore been most repugnant to most normal-minded people from the ancient patriarchs till now. God's rule for Israel, His Chosen People, has been indoga-mous. Modern Israel has been similarly directed.
>
> We are not unmindful of the fact that there is a growing tendency, particularly among some educators, as it mani-fests itself in this area, toward the breaking down of race barriers in the matter of intermarriage between white and blacks, but it does not have the sanction of the Church and is contrary to Church doctrine.[178]

Brigham Young made a very strong statement on this matter when he said, "I would like the President of the United States and all the world to hear this. Shall I tell you the law of God in regard to the African race? If the white man who belongs to the CHOSEN SEED mixes his blood with the seed of Cain, the penalty under the law of God, is death on the spot. This will always be so."[179] God has commanded Israel not to intermarry.[180] To go against this commandment of God would be to sin. Those who willfully sin with their eyes open to this wrong will not be surprised to find that they will be separated from the presence of God in the world to come. This is spirit-ual death.

President Joseph F. Smith has said, "I would rather go myself to the grave than to be associated with a wife outside of the bonds of the new and everlasting cove-nant."[181] Let Negroes marry Negroes and let whites marry white and let every other race do the same. There will be Negroes, whites, and those of all races in the Celestial Kingdom if each will follow the commandments of God. All can be assured, however, that no one who rebels against the order of heaven will ever be allowed to live there.

In the Bible it is written that the Lord warned Israel not to intermarry. ". . . thou shalt make no covenant with them . . . Neither shalt thou make marriages with them; thy daughters thou shalt not give unto his son, nor his daughter shalt thou take unto they son."[182] "It displeased the Lord when the 'sons of God,' in Noah's day, began to marry the 'daughters of men.' (Gen. 6:2-3) Esau grieved his parents by marrying Hittite women. (Gen. 26: 34-35) Samson's father asked his son why he sought after those outside their own people. (Jud. 14:3)"[184] Did not Abraham who was one of the Chosen of the Lord send his servant into a far off land to find a wife for his son because he did not want him to marry a daughter of the Canaanites?[185] It was because of the sin of intermarriage that the Prophet Ezra rent his clothes as a sign of mourning for as he said to the Lord, ". . . the holy seed have mingled themselves . . ."[186] and ". . . have forsaken thy commandments."[187]

Certainly there are few on the earth today who could claim a pure lineage unspotted by interracial marriage. However, this does not change the fact that it is still against the commandments of God. In regard to intermarriage with the Negro, all must be similarly warned. God does not approve! Brigham Young admonished, "Be careful, O ye mothers in Israel, and do not teach your daughters in the future, as many of them have been taught, to marry out of Israel. Wo to you who do it; you will lose your crowns as sure as God lives."[188]

The reason that one would lose his blessings by marrying a Negro is due to the restriction placed upon them. "No person having the least particle of Negro blood can hold the Priesthood."[189] It does not matter if they are one-sixth Negro or one-one hundred and sixth, the curse of no Priesthood is still the same. If an individual who is entitled to the Priesthood marries a Negro, the Lord has decreed that only spirits who are not eligible for the Priesthood will come to that marriage as children. To intermarry with a Negro is to forfeit a "Nation of Priesthood holders."[190]

FOOTNOTES

[170]Psalms 33:12.

[171]McConkie, *Mormon Doctrine, op. cit.*, p. 554.

[172]Abraham 3:22.

[173]Abraham 3:23.

[174]Jer. 1:5.

[175]*Teachings of the Prophet Joseph Smith, op. cit.*, p. 365.

[176]McConkie, *Mormon Doctrine, op. cit.*, p. 435.

[177]David O. McKay in Berrett's "The Church and the Negroid People," *Mormonism and the Negro, op. cit.*, p. 22.

[178]Stewart, *Mormonism and the Negro, op. cit.*, p. 47.

[179]Brigham Young, *Journal of Discourses*, 10:110-11.

[180]Deut. 7:3.

[181]N. B. Lundwall (comp.), *The Vision* (Salt Lake City, Utah: Bookcraft) p. 154.

[182]Deut. 7:3.

[183]I Kings 11:2-3.

[184]Brooks, *L.D.S. Reference Encyclopedia, op. cit.*, p. 289.

[185]Gen. chapter 24.

[186]Ezra 9:1-3.

[187]Ezra 9:10.

[188]Lundwall, *The Vision, op. cit.*, pp. 152-53.

[189]Cowley, *Wilford Woodruff, op. cit.*, p. 351, citing Brigham Young.

[190]Hunter, *Pearl of Great Price Commentary, op. cit.*, p. 201.

VII

WHAT IS THE STATUS OF THE NEGRO IN THE MORMON CHURCH?

A NOTHER CONSIDERATION OF THIS BOOK IS THE STATUS OF the Negro in the Church of Jesus Christ of Latter-day Saints. Joseph Fielding Smith, when he was the President of the Quorum of the Twelve, wrote in *Answers to Gospel Questions* the following article concerning the status of the Negro:

> When uninformed people, speaking of political and other matters, undertake to interpret the position of The Church of Jesus Christ of Latter-day Saints with respect to the status of the Negro, they do the Church a grave injustice and present views which are not correct. . . .
>
> The ignorance on the part of writers who do not belong to The Church of Jesus Christ of Latter-day Saints in relation to the view of the "Mormons" on the status religiously or otherwise of the Negro in inexcusable. . . . The Latter-day Saints, so commonly called "Mormons," have no animosity toward the Negro. Neither have they described him as belonging to an "inferior race." There are Negroes in the Church who are respected and honored for their integrity and faithful devotion. The door into the Church is open to all. One ancient Nephite prophet wrote the following:
>
>> And again, the Lord hath commanded that men should not murder; that they should not lie; that they should not steal; that they should not take the name of the Lord their God in vain; that they should not envy; that they should not have malice; that they should not contend one with another; that they should not commit whoredoms; and that they should do none of these things; for whoso doeth them shall perish.
>>
>> For none of these iniquities come of the Lord; for he doeth that which is good among the children of men; and he doeth nothing save it be plain unto the children of men; and he inviteth them all to come unto him and

partake of his goodness; and he denieth none that come unto him, black and white, bond and free, male and female; and he remembereth the heathen; and all are alike unto God both Jew and Gentile. (II Nephi 26:32-33.)

The Church can do More for the Negro

Moreover, according to the faith and knowledge of the elders of The Church of Jesus Christ of Latter-day Saints, who are so frequently called "Mormons," the Church can do more for the Negro than any other church on the face of the earth. What other church can baptize them by divine authority and confirm them and give them the gift of the Holy Ghost? What other church can promise them with assurance that they can, if they are faithful and true before the Lord, enter into the celestial kingdom? Not one of them! For other churches do not know anything about the celestial kingdom.

Paul has revealed to the world through the doctrine he taught the Corinthian Saints, that there are three kingdoms, or glories, into which mankind will go. These are the words of Paul:

> All flesh is not the same flesh: but there is one kind of flesh of men, another flesh of beasts, another of fishes, and another of birds.
>
> There are also celestial bodies, and bodies terrestrial: but the glory of the celestial is one, and the glory of the terrestrial is another.
>
> There is one glory of the sun, and another glory of the moon, and another glory of the stars; for one star differeth from another star in glory.
>
> So also is the resurrection of the dead. It is sown in corruption; it is raised in incorruption. (I Corinthians 15:39-42.)

Negroes May Become Heirs of the Celestial Kingdom

Therefore if a Negro joins the Church through the waters of baptism and is confirmed by the laying on of hands and then he remains faithful and true to the teachings of the Church and in keeping the commandments the Lord has given, he will come forth in the first resurrection and will enter the celestial kingdom of God.

What other church can make a better promise? Moreover we know whereof we speak, for the gospel of Jesus Christ has been restored with all its powers and divine authority.

The Negro who accepts the doctrines of the Church and is baptized by an authorized minister of The Church of Jesus Christ of Latter-day Saints is entitled to salvation in the celestial kingdom or the highest heaven spoken of by Paul. It is true that the work of the ministry is given to other peoples and why should the so-called Christian denominations complain? How many Negroes have been placed as ministers over white congregations in the so-called Christian denominations? It appears that a great deal of noise has been made over a problem that does not really exist or is not peculiar to the Latter-day Saints[191]

The fact that Negroes may join the Church is undeniable. It has been the privilege of this author to baptize several Negroes into the Church and to personally confer membership upon their heads by the power of the Holy Priesthood. "Negroes may be baptized, and we have many Negroes in the Church."[192]

WHAT CAN A NEGRO DO ONCE HE IS A MEMBER OF THE MORMON CHURCH?

ONCE A NEGRO IS A MEMBER OF THE MORMON CHURCH he is entitled to all the blessings of a worthy member and, if faithful, may be called upon to serve in numerous positions of responsibility.

Teacher

A worthy member, whether Negroid or not may be called to teach a religious class in any of the auxiliary organizations of the Church. This may include a class in the *Primary Organizations,* a group which teaches children from the ages of three to twelve the fundamentals of our religion. The *Junior and Senior Sunday Schools* also have various positions for teachers which could be filled by

Negroes. *The Mutual Improvement Association,* an organization that meets once a week is primarily a young people's group for those from twelve years of age and older. A worthy member might be called to serve in a variety of capacities in the MIA: as a teacher, scout master, dance instructor, drama coach, sports director, or music director. *The Relief Society* is an organization of women that meets once a week for instruction in culture and literature, theology, social science, and domestic arts. A Negress could be one of the teachers in this organization.

Administrator

The Church is divided into stakes, missions, wards and branches. The basic unit is either a ward or a branch which may vary in membership from a few to a thousand. A congregation of three to four hundred would be typical of an established ward. Stakes are made up of a number of wards. A Negro, if called, could serve as the superintendent of the ward or stake Sunday School program or the president of the ward or stake MIA, Primary, or Relief Society organizations. He or she could also serve as a counselor to the president in any of these organizations.

Other Postions

There are other positions in the various organizations that a Negro may be called to fill such as a chorister, organist, choir director, Church magazine representative, genealogical worker, and a host of other assignments which are made to members to make a ward function properly.

INDIVIDUAL ACTIVITIES
OF THE TYPICAL MEMBER

THERE IS NO PAID MINISTRY IN THE CHURCH OF JESUS Christ of Latter-day Saints and consequently the task of praying, teaching, and giving sermons is left to the membership.

Praying

A Mormon Negro may be called on to pray for the entire congregation in a religious or social gathering.

Sacrament

A worthy member is expected to partake of the Sacrament every Sunday in remembrance of his baptismal covenants.

Give Sermons

Sermons, commonly known as "talks" in the LDS Church, are given by the membership in Sunday School and Sacrament service as well as other meetings. It would not be unusual to call upon a worthy Negro member to prepare and deliver a sermon for the edification of the entire congregation. Many Negro members are called upon to speak at firesides and other friendly gatherings where people meet in the name of Christ. In seminaries and institutes of religion Negro members are often requested to give special lectures. Brother A. L. Howell, a Negro member tells us:

> I spoke to many firesides and seminaries and University of Southern California Institute. President Paul Dunn said I could please his classes better than he could, sometimes, as they liked to see me come. I spoke to several of Brother Tingey's classes. I talked to a class of Brother William Heartman in Long Beach, that had no standing room, all wanting to know why I was a Mormon.[193]

Patriarchal Blessings

A Patriarchal blessing is a pronouncement of blessings given to worthy members of the Church. They are different for each individual and are considered most sacred. For this reason, Patriarchal blessings are not generally circulated. It should be pointed out that they are not secret but sacred. Worthy Mormon Negroes may receive a Patriarchal blessing. A member of the First Presidency has said that any Negro ". . . if he should truly repent may be baptized and come into the Church and have a patriarchal blessing. Some Negroes who are members of the Church have received patriarchal blessings."[194] The author has read part of a patriarchal blessing given to a Mormon Negro by the name of Samuel Chambers who received his blessing at the hands of Patriarch Smith.[195] Brother Chambers is now dead, having died in 1925, and because of the sacred nature of the blessing it is felt that it would not be proper to publish it in a work of this sort. The point is, however, that Negroes may receive a patriarchal blessing.

Entering the Temple

A myth that has been widely circulated is that Negroes cannot be allowed in a Mormon temple for any reason. This is false. A worthy Negro member may enter the temple and be baptized vicariously for the dead.[196] They cannot, however, be endowed or sealed.

Serve As A Missionary

Negro members of the Church can, if called, serve as missionaries preaching the gospel to the inhabitants of this world. Elijah Abel, a Negro member, served a mission for the LDS Church in Canada. (See the case of Elijah Abel.) They may teach, instruct, warn, call to repentance, and do whatsoever is needful but they cannot function in a capacity that requires Priesthood.

Vote

Every member has the opportunity at least once a year in his ward of voting to sustain those who have been called to serve over him. It is not an election but a vote of support or non-support for those who have been called to serve. Negro members may vote.

WHAT IS WORTHY MEMBERSHIP?

THE POINT HAS BEEN MENTIONED SEVERAL TIMES THAT involvement in the previous activities depends on worthy membership. Briefly the author will attempt to describe what things an active Mormon would do to be classified as a worthy member. This includes Negroes as well.

Attend Meetings

A worthy member is one who attends faithfully his Sunday meetings and supports the other auxiliaries such as the MIA or Relief Society as much as possible.

Tithing

A worthy member will pay one-tenth of all he earns to the Lord. This tithing money is used primarily for building and educational purposes.

Support Authorities

A worthy member will support the persons who have been placed in authority over him. If asked to serve in a position of responsibility he will accept, realizing that he will be required to sacrifice time and effort in fulfilling that position.

Morally Clean

A worthy member is one whose life is a shining example of virtuous living. He is clean, pure and wholesome in his relationships with others and does not become involved in any way with sexual sins.

Obey the Word of Wisdom

A worthy member obeys the Word of Wisdom. Specifically, this means that the individual refrains from doing anything that would harm his body. This means no smoking or chewing of tobacco, no drinking of alcoholic beverages or intoxicating drinks of any kind, no drinking of coffee or tea, and in general refraining from anything that would affect one's body adversely.

Prayer

A worthy member is one who is in contact with God through daily individual prayer, family prayer, and returning grace over the food.

Fasting

A worthy member is expected to fast once a month. This entails going without food for twenty-four hours and donating that money which would have been spent on food to the poor.

Family Home Evening

A worthy member is expected to hold a family home evening. This consists of gathering the family together at least once a week to instruct them in the principles of the Gospel.

The foregoing requirements for worthy membership are the minimal standards. Those who would be worthy members are encouraged to live exemplary lives of Christian love and service.

OTHER CHURCHES

THE MORMON CHURCH WILL CHALLENGE ANY RELIGIOUS organization in the world to provide a similar list of activities and responsibilities for their membership whether Negroid or white. As stated in the beginning of this section, " 'Mormons' . . . can do more for the Negro than any other church on the face of the earth."[197]

SUMMARY ON STATUS OF THE NEGRO

IT IS TRUE THAT THE NEGRO IS NOT ENTITLED TO THE Priesthood in the Mormon Church. The worthy Mormon Negro, however, is entitled to function as a teacher, administrator and active member. There is much that the Negro can do. He is able to be baptized, confirmed, partake of the sacrament, pray for the congregation, deliver sermons, receive a Patriarchal blessing, enter the temple to be baptized for the dead, serve as a missionary, attend meetings in a non-segregated chapel and sustain the officers in the Church by raising the right hand. Again we repeat—the Mormon Church can do more for the Negro than any other church on the face of the earth!

FOOTNOTES

[191]Joseph Fielding Smith, *Answers to Gospel Questions, op. cit.*, 4:169-72.

[192]Joseph Fielding Smith, *Doctrines of Salvation, op. cit.*, II:55.

[193]Kate B. Carter (comp.), *Our Pioneer Heritage* (Salt Lake City, Utah: Daughters of Utah Pioneers, 1965), 8:556.

[194]Joseph Fielding Smith, *Doctrines of Salvation, op. cit.*, III:172.

[195]Carter, *Our Pioneer Heritage, op. cit.*, pp. 548-49.

[196]Personal interview with a temple president.

[197]Joseph Fielding Smith, *Answers to Gospel Questions, op. cit.*, 4:170-71.

VIII

COMMENTS BY AND ABOUT
MORMON NEGROES

T HIS SECTION PERTAINS TO NEGRO CONVERTS TO THE
Church and how they view their membership.
Comments by prominent Church leaders about Negro
members are also included.

JOHN LAMB—1966

I N AN ARTICLE PUBLISHED IN THE JANUARY 1966, *Improvement Era*, John Lamb, a Mormon Negro, made known
his feelings about not holding the Priesthood:

> To make a long story short, I was baptized into The
> Church of Jesus Christ of Latter-day Saints, received the
> Holy Ghost, and was accepted into membership.
>
> "But John Lamb," everyone I met seemed to ask, "what
> about the priesthood? You are a Negro! You were really
> brainwashed by those Mormons, weren't you?"
>
> And my answer was, and still is: "I know this to be the
> inspired, restored Gospel of Jesus Christ, not through blind
> faith, but through a knowledge that I have gained from our
> Heavenly Father."
>
> My position in this restored Church reminds me of the
> parable of the talents. Two men received more than one
> talent each and multiplied them in their lord's absence.
> Another man hid his talent. All of them were responsible
> for increasing their talents.
>
> Men now holding the Priesthood have a talent. For the
> present, God has given me other talents. It is my duty as a
> member of the Church to render service in every way I
> possibly can, to increase the talents I have been given. I
> am not excused and neither is a Priesthood holder.

My brothers and sisters, we are eligible for the blessings of the restored Gospel of Jesus Christ. I pray we will ever make ourselves worthy to receive them.[198]

LEN HOPE

ELDER MARK E. PETERSEN WROTE THE FOLLOWING:

Some years ago, . . . I became acquainted with a Negro family in Cincinnati, Ohio. I was back there for three months in connection with a newspaper assignment. I went to church and became acquainted with the family of a Negro man named Len Hope. Accidentally he had found some of our tracts when he lived down in Mississippi. He read them and became interested. He wrote to the mission headquarters for a Book of Mormon, and by his own study, converted himself. Later he met the Elders and joined the Church. Then he joined the army in the First World War. When he came back, having carried a Book of Mormon with him all through the war and studied it carefully, he converted his sweetheart whom he married, and she was baptized. . . .

They were very faithful people. Brother Hope died just a little while ago. He was a man who was as thoroughly converted to the Gospel as anyone I know. He was a full tithe payer all through the depression. He earned the most meager kind of living, but he never failed to pay his tithing. The branch president showed me the tithing records, and all through the depression Brother Hope paid $1.50 a week. It was a full tithing. Sometimes Brother Hope didn't even have that, so he went into the hills and picked berries and sold them on the streets of Cincinnati to get enough money to pay that $1.50 tithing.

Brother Hope told me, as a testimony, that in the Negro area of Cincinnati where he lived during the depression he didn't know of one man who had a job. But he said, "I had a job. I paid my tithing and during that whole depression, I didn't lose one day's work. Sometimes I didn't make much money on that day, and I did have to go out into the hills and get berries, but I always had an income."[199]

TWO TESTIMONIES

I N THE EARLY DAYS OF MORMON HISTORY, THERE WERE many Negro members of the Church who were well acquainted with the Prophet Joseph Smith and Brigham Young. Two of their testimonies follow:

> Isaac Manning bore a strong testimony concerning the Prophet. He said he knew Brother Joseph was a man of God, and he would have laid down his life for the prophet if he could have done so. He hoped to live so that he could meet the Prophet and be with him on the other side.[200]

> Green Flake . . . was a faithful Latter-day Saint, and to his dying day bore testimony to the divine mission of the Prophet Joseph Smith, with whose family he lived for a number of years prior to the Prophet's assassination. . . .[201]

EDGAR WHITTINGHAM—1965

E DGAR WHITTINGHAM, A STUDENT AT BYU, A MORMON university, related his story about being a Mormon Negro, to a sociology class in the fall of 1964. In the spring of 1965, it was the privilege of this author to listen to essentially the same presentation at a fireside talk in Orem, Utah.

> I was born in the Panama Canal Zone. After my parents died, when I was a little boy, I moved over to Panama City, the capital city of the Republic of Panama, where I learned to speak both English and Spanish. By way of background, you will recall that an agreement was made between Panama and the United States whereby a ten-mile strip of land on each side of the canal on a 40-mile length was granted to the United States in perpetuity. The Indians at that time were not willing to work and neither were the Spaniards, so they had to recruit other people to do some of the work. Many Negroes from the neighboring islands of Jamaica, and the West Indies in general, and some from Africa were recruited for the work. My grandparents were among those workers recruited. My mother was born in

Panama and my father migrated there. Through my mother, I am a third generation of Negroes now established in Panama.

My life has been mostly uneventful, but after graduation from high school I felt a need for more education. I decided to come to one of the schools here in the United States. Being a member of the Methodist Church, I naturally wanted to come to a Methodist school, but I found out that I couldn't afford to, so after I graduated from high school I decided I would work and save my money and perhaps come up here later and investigate some of the different schools I was interested in. I went through the list of catalogs they had in one of the libraries in Panama and learned that Brigham Young University wasn't too far away and appeared to be a strong advocate of certain standards that I very much agreed with. Moreover, the tuition at BYU was low. I inquired at BYU and also at a couple of other schools. I received a more favorable response from BYU, so I decided to inquire a little more about this school, and I found out that it was a church school. Naturally, coming across a church school, if one did feel that there were any possibilities of going to this school in the future, he would investigate what the church stood for—its beliefs of doctrines. And this I went on to do, and I found out many things about the Church.

I would say that perhaps 90 percent of the people in Panama do not know much about Mormonism, or did not at that time, three years ago. Very few of us knew anything about Mormonism. I had never heard the word "Mormon." At any rate, I went out and visited one of the branches that they had down in the Canal Zone, and I was very much amazed at what I saw. I went back frequently to visit the Church, and I learned much about it. This, of course, led to a conflict with the Methodist church, where I was teaching in Sunday School and had several other responsibilities, because my interests in Mormonism caused me to delegate my responsibilities to somebody else and attend the Mormon Church. Of course, it was proper for them to call my attention to my neglect of duty, but the way they did it angered me very much; so, feeling that I had the right to make my own choice, I continued to go to the Mormon Church. This went on for several months and eventually there was a complete split between the Methodist Church and myself. I then continued to go to the Mormon Church exclusively.

It was approximately eight months after my first meeting with the Mormons that I made one of the major decisions of my life. Studying the Gospel teachings of the Church, I found out many things that I had never known before. I found that Mormon doctrine conformed with many of the principles I had learned in Christianity; I felt that this church had much more to offer and they were living much closer to the principles of the Church of the Gospel than any other religion that I had read about or had been acquainted with up until that time. They showed me new ways of applying the teachings of Christ in one's daily life. And so naturally I felt that I would like to become part of this organization because I felt that it would do much more for me and perhaps even for my people.

When I made it known that I had decided to take steps to become a member of the Church, my friend, the person who actually taught me the Gospel or discussed it with me or explained most of its features to me, very hesitatingly approached me one day and said that he had something very special to tell me. Then he proceeded to explain the curse on the Negroes. Naturally I was deeply hurt and greatly upset about it. I guess my emotions got the best of me. I didn't do anything irrational, but having been deeply wounded in the house of my friends, I left the Church and stayed away for approximately a year. During this period of emotional distress I was going with the girl who is now my wife. Today she's a member of the Church and she's also Negro, but she was then a member of the Baptist Church. I used to attend church with her. I also had friends who were members of the Jehovah Witness group and they worked on me to see religion from their point of view. Thus I continued to have opportunities to weigh Mormonism against the teachings of other churches. In time I gradually overcame the emotional hurt and after much reflective thinking, I returned to the LDS branch.

I joined the Church and made application to BYU. I was told that I did not have sufficient funds to come and so I worked another year as a clerk-typist in Panama and saved enough money and applied again the following year and was accepted. I came to BYU about three years ago and I expect to return home after I complete my studies.

My experiences here at the "Y" for the most part have been most favorable. I have never had much opportunity to travel, and it's hard for me to make comparisons, but from what I can gather I would say that most of the students here have been very friendly, very open-minded, and I've had very little difficulty in my dealings with others. As a Negro, of course, I do find that it's hard to say exactly whenever I have difficulty whether it has to do with myself as a person or has to do with the race. The difficulties and problems that I've had have seemed rather minor and I have just sort of brushed them aside as incidental. I know that I'm not the most agreeable person to be with or sometimes to deal with and, therefore, there are occasions when people might just dislike me on a personality basis.

This is a major emphasis I want to make. I think a person should be judged on his merits and his personality rather than as a member of a race. Whatever I say today, for instance, in no way reflects the opinions of other Negroes, even Negroes who are members of the Church. . . . Negroes are people. They are individuals. You can find just about any kind of Negro that you can find among your own friends. You can find them intelligent, good, bad, honest, or dishonest. I think it is unfair and wrong to group people and say, well, all Negroes are such and such or all Negroes do this or that. We're all different in many respects. We may have many similarities. We may have many common things, but we all have different personalities. We enjoy associating with people who have the same interests we have, but there is no justification for prejudices or for discrimination because of color. . . .

Talks About the Priesthood

In what I have said here today I have not tried to make everybody happy or to agree with your personal feelings because you are members of the Church. I am also a member of the Church, and I think even among us we have differences. We have our own personal beliefs on some of the doctrines that we have heard. Up until the time I was told that because I was a Negro I could not hold the Priesthood, my knowledge of Christianity in the Methodist

Church had persuaded me to believe that regardless of color
we would all have the opportunity to do the same things or
acquire the same glories. My reaction to being told I could
not hold the priesthood was that it was a stigma of discrimination. Now this is the general belief that I think most
Negroes hold today. Perhaps the only reason I am a member
of the Church today is that I heard the Gospel before I had
known of this particular curse. I don't know whether I
could have been objective enough or open-minded enough
to have gone through with my study of the teachings of the
Church if I had known the Church position concerning
Negroes and Priesthood.

I've had contact with many Negroes since joining the
Church who have not pursued their interests in the Church
because they were repelled by awareness of inability to
acquire full Priesthood fellowship. Even as a member of the
Church, I still find the "curse" very difficult to understand.
I find others also have difficulty understanding this problem.
. . . I have talked to many people also about the idea that
we Negroes were cursed in the pre-existence. It is argued
that we may have done something in the pre-existence that
may have hurt our personal growth. . . . I do know that the
Church has a right to receive revelation, and I believe that
through revelation a change may be made. . . . Whether
or not Negroes will receive the Priesthood during my life
I don't know, but it has been said that the Negro who proves
worthy will receive the Priesthood some time. . . . God
loves us, and He is just. In due time we will all receive
the rewards we merit. In the meantime we must search and
hope. . . .

I am grateful for all that has come to me, and I trust
my future to God's care. If I continue to try to seek for
truth it will come, and in God's own time I believe I shall
be able to receive the Priesthood if I am worthy. . . .[202]

EARLY MORMON NEGROES

MORMON NEGROES HAVE BEEN CLOSELY ASSOCIATED
with Church History since the time of the Prophet
Joseph Smith. Many of these Negroes came west with the
Mormon Pioneers. A brief history of a few of these Ne-

groes reveals that they have been among the most faithful in the Church.

Jane Manning James

Jane Manning James was born May 11, 1813, in New Hampshire. She became a convert to Mormonism and within a short time after her conversion moved to Nauvoo where she became a servant in the home of the Prophet Joseph Smith. She married Sherman James, whom she had known in Connecticut and who had followed her to Nauvoo. The family was listed in the Ira Eldredge Company, some of the first pioneers. They arrived in Utah in 1848, as members of Brigham Young's household. Anne Shipp, who was a young girl at the time "Auntie Jane" lived in Salt Lake gave the following testimonial of the faithfulness of this woman:

> My parents and family moved from Manti to Salt Lake City in 1901 and located in the Third Ward. Each Sunday I remember seeing two Negroes sitting on the stand and of being told they had both been servants in the home of the Prophet Joseph Smith. They were very old and their skin looked like parchment, but they appeared to be strong and well. Jane Manning James and her brother Isaac were given the seats of honor, and I have heard them tell of the time they lived with the Prophet. They were devoted Latter-day Saints, and everyone in the Third Ward loved and respected them.[203]

Eliza Lyman, wife of Amasa Lyman, tells this little story of Jane:

> April 8th, 1849, we baked the last of our flour today, and have no prospect of getting more till after harvest. April 13th Brother Lyman started on a mission to California . . . He left us without anything from which to make bread, it not being in his power to get it. Not long after Amasa had gone, Jane James, the colored woman, let me have two pounds of flour, it being half of what she had.[204]

Jane and her brother, Isaac, were members of the Mormon Church for nearly sixty-five years. The ward members tenderly referred to them as Aunt Jane and

Uncle Isaac. During many of those years they were the personal servants of President Brigham Young as well as Joseph Smith. Each "remained loyal and true to the Prophet's memory since his tragic death. . . . They were converted to Mormonism in the early 'forties' in Connecticut. Few persons were more noted for faith and faithfulness . . . and though of the humble of the earth . . . numbered friends and acquaintances by the hundreds."[205]

When "Aunt Jane" was laid to rest the meetinghouse "was crowded, many in the congregation being of her own race. Flowers in profusion were contributed by friends who had learned to respect the deceased for her undaunted faith and goodness of heart."[206]

Isaac Lewis Manning

Isaac Lewis Manning was the brother of Jane Manning James and was also a servant in the house of both the prophets, Joseph Smith and Brigham Young. He was born May 31, 1815, in Connecticut. He was baptized in 1835, and moved to Nauvoo. Isaac was married and had one child but his wife and child both died before he came to Utah. This information appeared in the Editor *News* at the time of his death:

> . . . He [Isaac] went to work for the Prophet Joseph Smith as cook in the Prophet's family at the Mansion House until it was closed. He worked at the stone quarry, getting out rock for the temple. Isaac also worked for William Huntington, the sexton, and dug two graves in the cemetery (these graves were dug to deceive the mob) for the bodies of the martyred Prophet and Patriarch. Isaac then dug two graves in the cellar of the Prophet Joseph's dwelling house, on the banks near the river; these graves were dug in the center of the cellar and the bodies were buried there. The graves in the cemetery had two coffins buried in them, filled with something heavy and a guard kept over the graves, but the remains of the brothers were buried elsewhere. Isaac stood guard half of each night, watching the mob. . . .[207]

President Joseph F. Smith, who spoke at the funeral of Isaac Manning, said that his faithfulness and his obedience to the gospel "placed him in a position to be a partaker of the blessings that God has in store for the faithful" and referred to the salvation that awaits all of God's children in the hereafter.[208] In Isaac's obituary it was written:

> . . . he was treated with a great deal of deference by all the Church officials and was respected and revered by all who knew him for his kind disposition and generous nature. He and his sister for years had special seats reserved for them in the tabernacle near the front in the center of the building. Jane made cushions for the seats, and the old couple and their friends had the exclusive right to the seats. Mr. Manning lived in the days of slavery, but was never in bondage. This fact always gave him great pleasure, and he claimed to be a regular New England Yankee.[209]

Samuel Chambers—1870

Samuel Chambers, a large mulatto with straight white hair, affectionately remembered in the old LDS Wilford Ward area as Brother Chambers, or Sam, was born in Louisiana, May 21, 1834, to a Negro mother and a Danish father. He saw his mother sold into slavery when he was a young boy. He married, and soon after the birth of his son, Peter, his wife died. May 10, 1864, Samuel married Amanda, a colored woman who was always loyal and devoted to her husband and the Church. Baptized by Mormon missionaries while in Mississippi, Samuel and his family traveled to Utah in 1870 with a group of colored Latter-day Saint converts.

Samuel acquired twenty acres of land . . . near Thirty-third South in Salt Lake City, where he and Amanda planted large and small fruit trees, alfalfa and a garden. . . . He and Amanda would sit under the currant bushes and pick the fruit, then while sitting under large black umbrellas, carefully clean them. Their best customers were the general authorities of the Church. The President always received from Sam and Amanda a basket-gift of canned and fresh fruit and vegetables at Christmas time. . . .

Samuel and Amanda were very devout members of the Church. He kept the Word of Wisdom faithfully and paid an honest and generous tithing, being the largest tithe payer in Wilford Ward for a long time. On one occasion, when Wilford Ward members were contemplating adding an amusement hall and classrooms to the old chapel . . . President Joseph F. Smith attended the conference to encourage the members in their endeavors. Samuel had offered the substantial sum of $1,000.00 to the building fund. After President Smith had delivered his address to the congregation, he turned to Brother Chambers, who occupied his usual place, the front bench on the south side of the chapel, and said, "I want to say a word to this good brother. There are not words to express or ways to tell the great blessings that await this faithful man, and he shall some day stand at the head of his race."[210]

Green Flake—Teamster

Green was born in January, 1825, in Anson County, North Carolina on the plantation of John Flake. He took his master's name and became known as Green Flake. He was baptized a member of the Latter-day Saint Church in the Mississippi River and went with the Flake family to Nauvoo, Illinois. Later, when Brigham Young was fitting out the first wagon train to cross the plains and needed the best teams, J. M. Flake, who had put his all on the alter, sent his slave, Green, with a team of white mules of which he was very proud. This team pulled a carriage to help the company to their destination. From family diaries and the memory of a grandson who is still living, it is believed that it was this carriage and team which Green drove that brought President Brigham Young to the valley.[211]

THE CASE OF ELIJAH ABEL

H ISTORY RECORDS AN INCIDENT OF ELIJAH ABEL, A Negro, being given the Priesthood. It should be understood however, that when the Church leaders became aware that this man had Negro blood, his Priesthood was suspended until that time when it will be proper in the eyes of the Lord for him to exercise this right.

In Andrew Jensen's *LDS Biographical Encyclopedia*, the following account of this incident is given:

Elijah Abel, the only colored man who is known to have been ordained to the Priesthood, was born July 25, 1810, in

Maryland. Becoming a convert to Mormonism he was baptized in September, 1832, by Ezekiel Roberts and, as appears from certificates, he was ordained an Elder March 3, 1836, and Seventy April 4, 1841. . . . At Nauvoo, Illinois, where he resided, he followed the avocation of an undertaker. After his arrival in Salt Lake City, he became a resident of the Tenth Ward and, together with his wife he managed the Farnham Hotel (later called the Denver House) in Salt Lake City. . . . In 1883, as a member of the Third Quorum of Seventy, he left Salt Lake City on a mission to Canada, during which he also performed missionary labors in the United States. Two weeks after his return he died, December 25, 1884, of debility, consequent upon exposure while laboring in the ministry in Ohio. He died in full faith of the Gospel."[212]

That Elijah Abel was a good man is not in question. The fact that he held the Priesthood is also a matter of record. But, as mentioned, the record needs to be clarified in a very major point. Once it was discovered that Elijah Abel was of Negroid ancestry, he was dropped from his Priesthood Quorum (1879).[213] He remained, however, a member in good standing and later served a mission (1883) as Negroes are allowed to do though they cannot function with the Priesthood.

It is obvious that when Joseph Smith said, "No person having the least particle of Negro blood can hold the Priesthood," that is exactly what he meant.[214] This was the situation in Elijah Abel's case. A quote from Berrett's supplement to *Mormonism and the Negro* reveals that Elijah was "one-eighth Negro and light of color."[215] Nevertheless, he did have Negro blood and was therefore not eligible for the Priesthood. Berrett also explains in referring to the entry cited in Jensen's *LDS Biographical Encyclopedia,*

> The entry is misleading because it does not disclose that Elijah Abel was only part Negro and does not disclose the fact that in a meeting, May 31, 1879, at the home of President A. O. Smoot, Provo, Utah, leaders of the Church reapproved that the Priesthood was not for the Negro, and that Elijah Abel was not to exercise any Priesthood rights.

The fact that subsequent to that date Elijah Abel was called on a mission does not necessarily imply that he participated in any baptisms or ordinations."[216]

It is also apparently true that several other Negroes, including some of Elijah Abel's descendants, have been ordained to the Priesthood. It is the policy of the Church in these and other cases to suspend the Priesthood from those who are known to be of the seed of Cain. It is admitted that the Priesthood has been mistakenly given to some Negroes who are light of color. However, the Church wishes to follow the order of heaven and the commandments of God; therefore, when Negro ancestry is discovered in a man who holds the Priesthood, he is suspended in the use of that Priesthood. It should be emphasized he maintains full fellowship in the Church, but is simply restricted in his use of the Priesthood.

FOOTNOTES

[198]John Lamb, "My Responsibility," *The Improvement Era*, LXIV, (January, 1966), 37.

[199]Carter, *Our Pioneer Heritage, op. cit.*, 8:557-58.

[200]*Ibid.*, 8:509.

[201]*Ibid.*, 8:502.

[202]Unpublished paper of Dr. Wilford S. Smith, "Is the Negro My Brother?" and author's firsthand account.

[203]Carter, *Our Pioneer Heritage, op. cit.*, 8:505.

[204]*Ibid.*, 8:505-506.

[205]*Ibid.*, 8:507.

[206]*Ibid.*

[207]*Ibid.*, 8:509.

[208]*Ibid.*, 8:508.

[209]*Ibid.*

[210]*Ibid.*, 8:547-48.

[211]*Ibid.*, 8:500-503.

[212]*Ibid.*, 8:511.

[213]Record in Church Historian's office.

[214]Berrett, "The Church and the Negroid People," *Mormonism and the Negro, op. cit.*, p. 10, Abraham O. Smoot citing Prophet Joseph Smith.

[215]*Ibid.*, p. 7.

[216]*Ibid.*, p. 8.

IX

CHURCH LEADERS SPEAK OUT ON THE NEGRO QUESTION

To those who think that the Church is silent on the issue of the Negro and the Priesthood this section is dedicated. It will be seen that almost every president of the Church as well as many apostles and other general authorities have commented on this question. From the early days of the Church up to and including the present the leaders of the Church have been frank and straightforward in presenting the Church's position concerning the Negro.

Joseph Smith

The Prophet's personal views were expressed when he proclaimed:

> Change their [Negro's] situation with the whites, and they would be like them. They have souls, and are subjects of salvation. Elder Hyde remarked, "Put them on the level, and they will rise above me." I replied, if I raise you to be my equal, and then attempted to oppress you, would you not be indignant and try to rise above me? . . . Had I anything to do with the Negro, I would confine them by strict law to their own species, and put them on a national equalization. (Joseph Smith, Jr., *History of the Church,* V:217-218.)

> They [Negroes] have souls, and are subjects of salvation. Go into Cincinnati or any city, and find an educated Negro . . . and you will see a man who has risen by the powers of his own mind to his state of respectability. The slaves in Washington are more refined than many in high places. . . . (Joseph Smith, Jr., *History of the Church,* V:217.)

During the early struggles of civil rights the Prophet Joseph made several comments on the status of the Negro in the United States. He made the following prophetic utterance on December 25, 1832, concerning a civil war

almost thirty years before the first shot was fired in South
Carolina:

> Verily, thus saith the Lord concerning the wars that will
> shortly come to pass, beginning at the rebellion of South
> Carolina, which will eventually terminate in the death and
> misery of many souls;
>
> And the time will come that war will be poured out
> upon all nations, beginning at this place.
>
> For behold, the Southern States shall be divided against
> the Northern States, and the Southern States will call on
> other nations, even the nation of Great Britain, as it is
> called, and they shall also call upon other nations, in order
> to defend themselves against other nations; and then war
> shall be poured out upon all nations.
>
> And it shall come to pass, after many days, slaves shall
> rise up against their masters, who shall be marshaled and
> disciplined for war. (Doctrine and Covenants 87:1-4)

On the issue of slavery Joseph Smith had much to say:

> . . . the Declaration of Independence "holds these truths to
> be self-evident, that all men are created equal; that they are
> endowed by their Creator with certain inalienable rights;
> that among these are life, liberty, and the pursuit of happi-
> ness," but at the same time, some two or three millions of
> people are held as slaves for life, because the spirit in them
> is covered with a darker skin than ours . . . the Constitution,
> when it says, "We, the people of the United States, in order
> to form a more perfect union, establish justice, ensure
> domestic tranquility, provide for the common defense, pro-
> mote the general welfare, and secure the blessings of liberty
> to ourselves and our posterity, do ordain and establish this
> this Constitution for the United States of America," meant
> just what it said without reference to color or condition, *ad
> infinitum.* (Clark, *Messages of the First Presidency,* I:19L-
> 92.)

> Petition, also, ye goodly inhabitants of the slave states,
> your legislators to abolish slavery by the year 1850, or now,
> and save the abolitionist from reproach and ruin, infamy
> and shame.

> Pray Congress to pay every man a reasonable price for
> his slaves out of the surplus revenue arising from the sale of
> public land, and from the deduction of pay from the mem-
> bers of Congress.

Break off the shackles from the poor black man, and hire him to labor like other human beings; for "an hour of virtuous liberty on earth is worth a whole eternity of bondage." (Clark, *Messages of the First Presidency*, I:199.)

The Prophet instructed Abraham O. Smoot to baptize the Negro but not confer the Priesthood upon him. (William E. Berrett, "The Church and the Negroid People," *Mormonism and the Negro*, p. 11.)

Brigham Young

(1854)

Cain conversed with his God every day, and knew all about the plan of creating this earth, for his father told him. But, for the want of humility, and through jealousy and an anxiety to possess the kingdom and to have the whole of it under his own control, and not allow anybody else the right to say one word, what did he do? He killed his brother. The Lord put a mark on him; and there are some of his children in this room. When all the other children of Adam have had the privilege of receiving the Priesthood, and of coming into the kingdom of God, and of being redeemed from the four quarters of the earth, and have received their resurrection from the dead, then it will be time enough to remove the curse from Cain and his posterity. He deprived his brother of the privilege of pursuing his journey through life, and of extending his kingdom by multiplying upon the earth; and because he did this, he is the last to share the joys of the kingdom of God.

Here are the Lamanites [Indians], another example. . . . Jesus revealed Himself to them after He was slain, preached to them the Gospel. But in the fourth generation the Priesthood was driven from their midst, and after that, the laws, ordinances, and power of the Gospel ceased to be with them. (*Journal of Discourses*, 2:142-143.)

(1855)

Formerly the rumor was that "they [Mormons] were agoing to tamper with the slaves," when we had never thought of such a thing. . . . I will here say a little more upon this point. The conduct of the whites towards the slaves will, in many cases, send both slave and master to hell. This statement comprises much in a few words. The

blacks should be used like servants, and not like brutes. . . .
It is their privilege to live so as to enjoy many of the bless-
ings which attend obedience to the first principles of the
Gospel, though they are not entitled to the Priesthood.
(*Journal of Discourses*, 2:184.)

(1859)

. . . The first man that committed the odious crime of
killing one of his brethren will be cursed the longest of
anyone of the children of Adam. Cain slew his brother.
Cain might have been killed, and that would have put a
termination to that line of human beings. This was not to be,
and the Lord put a mark upon him which is the flat nose
and black skin. Trace mankind down to after the flood, and
then another curse is pronounced upon the same race—that
they should be the "servant of servants;" and they will be,
until that curse is removed; and the abolitionist cannot help
it, nor in the least alter that decree. How long is that race
to endure the dreadful curse that is upon them? That curse
will remain upon them, and they never can hold the Priesthood or share in it until all the other descendants of Adam
have received the promises and enjoyed the blessings of the
Priesthood and the keys thereof. Until the last ones of the
residue of Adam's children are brought up to that favourable
[sic] position, the children of Cain cannot receive the first
ordinances of the Priesthood. They were the first that were
cursed, and they will be the last from whom the curse will
be removed. When the residue of the family of Adam come
up and receive their blessings, then the curse will be removed from the seed of Cain, and they will receive blessings
in like proportion. (*Journal of Discourses*, 7:290-291.)

(1863)

If the Government of the United States, in Congress
assembled, had the right to pass an anti-polygamy bill, they
had also the right to pass a law that slaves should not be
abused as they have been; they had also a right to make a
law that Negroes should be used like human beings, and not
worse than dumb brutes. For their abuse of that race, the
whites will be cursed, unless they repent.

I am neither an abolitionist nor a pro-slavery man.
(*Journal of Discourses*, 10:111.)

(1863)

What is the cause of all this waste of life and treasure [civil war]? To tell it in a plain, truthful way, one portion of the country wish to raise Negroes or black slaves, and the other portion wish to free them, and, apparently, to almost worship them. Well, raise and worship them, who cares? I should never fight one moment about it, for the cause of human improvement is not in the least advanced by the dreadful war which now convulses our unhappy country.

Ham will continue to be the servant of servants, as the Lord has decreed, until the curse is removed. Will the present struggle free the slave? No, but they are now wasting away the black race by thousands. Many of the blacks are treated worse than we treat our dumb brutes; and men will be called to judgment for the way they have treated the Negro, and they will receive the condemnation of a guilty conscience, by the just Judge whose attributes are justice and truth. (*Journal of Discourses*, 10:250.)

(1869)

President Brigham Young, answering a question put to him by Elder Lorenzo D. Young in a meeting held December 25, 1869, in Salt Lake City, said that Joseph Smith had declared that the Negroes were not neutral in heaven, for all the spirits took sides, but the "posterity of Cain are black because he [Cain] committed murder. But the spirits are pure (i.e., innocent. See Doctrine & Covenants 93:38) that enter their tabernacles and there will be a chance for the redemption of all the children of Adam, except the Sons of Perdition. (R. M. Frame, *The Negro Question*)

Parley P. Pratt

In regards to the pre-existence and the Priesthood, Parley P. Pratt said the following:

In organizing and peopling the worlds, it was found necessary to place among the inhabitants some superior intelligences, who were capacitated to teach, to rule, and preside among other intelligences. . . . Now the Lord did not predicate His principle of election or nobility upon . . . an unequal, unjust, and useless order of things. When He speaks of nobility, He simply means an election made, and an office or title conferred, on the principle of . . . nobleness of action, or of capacity to act. And when this election, with its titles, dignities, and estates, includes the unborn posterity of a chosen man, as in the case of Abraham, Isaac, and Jacob, it is with a view of the noble spirits of the eternal world coming through their lineage, and being taught in the commandments of God. Hence the prophets, kings, priests, patriarchs, apostles, and even Jesus Christ, were included in the election of Abraham, and of his seed, as manifested to him in an eternal covenant. . . .

Knowing of the covenants and promises made to the fathers, as I now know them and the rights of heirship to the Priesthood, as manifested in the election of God, I would never receive any man as an apostle or a priest, holding the keys of restoration, to bless the nations, while he claimed to be of any other lineage than Israel. (*Journal of Discourses*, 1:257-58, 262.)

Erastus Snow

Erastus Snow gives this explanation of the birthright of the Priesthood:

Cain . . . might have been the head of this Priesthood, under his father . . . but instead of exercising his birthright on the principles of righteousness, and in accord with the powers of heaven, he was befogged and understood not his true position; and his offering was not accepted. . . . When Cain found that his offering was not accepted, and his brother, Abel's, was accepted, Satan tempted him . . . he became possessed with the spirit of murder. . . . Cain lost his privilege [to the birthright of the Priesthood] . . . and the blessing fell on one more worthy, and the rights of the Priesthood passed to the next son of Adam, which according to Bible record was Seth, who magnified the Priesthood, honored his birthright, and held the blessing of the Priesthood, which was sealed upon him by his father; and from him it descended upon the righteous of his posterity.

There are many instances, from that time forward, of which the scriptures speak of this birthright continuing among the descendants of Seth, until it came to Noah and his sons, of which sons Shem received the blessings pertaining to the priesthood. Abraham came through Shem, and the Savior came through this lineage; and through this blessing of Noah upon Shem, the Priesthood continued through his seed; while the offspring of Ham inherited a curse, and it was because, as a revelation teaches, some of the blood of Cain became mingled with that of Ham's family, and hence they inherited that curse. (*Journal of Discourses*, 21:370.)

John Taylor

On the topic of civil rights, John Taylor stated as follows:

We must not . . . in the least seek to curtail any man in his individual rights. We wish it fully understood by the Saints and by all the world that we have a profound respect for all wholesome and constitutional laws. We are the firm and unequivocal advocates of law and order, and of every principle associated with human freedom . . . we are also fighting the battle of civil and religious liberty, and of freedom of conscience in behalf of our common humanity and in the interest of every people. (Clark, *Messages of the First Presidency*, III:80.)

John Taylor also gives an explanation of what happened to those people who would have come through the lineage of Abel: "To Eve God gave another seed in the place of Abel. 'For God, said she, hath appointed me another seed instead of Abel whom Cain slew.' [Gen. 4:25.] Who made this appointment? God . . ." (Clark, *Messages of the First Presidency*, III:66.)

Wilford Woodruff

Wilford Woodruff said about the Negro, "The day will come when all that race will be redeemed and possess all the blessings which we now have." (Berrett, "The Church and the Negroid People," *Mormonism and the Negro*, p. 16.)

In Matthew Cowley's book, *Wilford Woodruff*, the following story is told:

There is one peculiar characteristic noticeable in the journal of Wilford Woodruff, . . . he loved to dwell upon the good deeds of others . . . He said in his journal of October, that year, that "Aunt Jane," [Jane Manning James] the colored sister, had been to see him. She was anxious to go through the Temple and receive the higher ordinances of the Gospel. President Woodruff blessed her for her constant, never changing devotion to the Gospel, but explained to her her disadvantages as one of the descendants of Cain.

In after years when President Joseph F. Smith preached the funeral sermon of this same faithful woman he declared that she would in the resurrection attain the longing of her soul and become a white and beautiful person. (Matthew Cowley, *Wilford Woodruff*, p. 587.)

About the mark of Cain, Wilford Woodruff said, "What was that mark? It was a mark of blackness. That mark rested upon Cain, and descended upon his posterity from that time until the present. Today there are millions of the descendants of Cain, through the lineage of Ham, in the world, and that mark of darkness still rests upon them. (*Millennial Star*, 51:339.)

B. H. Roberts

B. H. Roberts gave an explanation of how the pre-existence relates to the Negro and his position on the earth:

From the Pearl of Great Price (pp. 7 and 32) we learn it was for seeking to destroy the agency of man, and for rebellion, that Lucifer and his followers were cast out of heaven. The contest was a severe one, and during its progress all degrees of integrity were manifest. Those who stood with Christ and the plan He favored for the salvation of man, formed one extreme, while those who stood with Lucifer and for the plan of salvation devised by him, which was destructive of man's agency, formed the other extreme; between these two extremes every shade of faith, fulness and indifference was exhibited. Only those, however, who wickedly rebelled against God were adjudged to deserve banishment from heaven, and become the devil and his angels. Others there were, who may not have rebelled against God, and yet were so indifferent in their support of the righteous cause of our Redeemer, that they forfeited certain privileges and powers granted to those who were more valiant for God and correct principle. We have, I think, a demonstration of this in the seed of Ham. The first Pharaoh—patriarch-king of Egypt—was a grandson of Ham:

and "being a righteous man, established his kingdom, and judged his people wisely and justly all his days, seeking earnestly to imitate that order established in the first generation, in the days of the first patriarchal reign, even in the reign of Adam, and also of Noah, his father, who blessed him with the blessings of the earth and with the blessings of wisdom, but who *cursed him as pertaining to the Priesthood.* He being of that lineage by which he could not have right to the Priesthood, notwithstanding the Pharaoh's would fain claim it from Noah through Ham." (Pearl of Great Price, p. 28.)

Now, why is it that the seed of Ham was cursed as pertaining to the Priesthood? Why is it that his seed "could not have right to the Priesthood?" Ham's wife was named "Egyptus, which in the Chaldaic signifies Egypt, which signifies that which is forbidden: ° ° and thus from Ham sprang that race which preserved the curse in the land." (Pearl of Great Price, p. 28.) Was the wife of Ham, as her name signifies, of a race with which those who held the Priesthood were forbidden to intermarry? Was she a descendant of Cain, who was cursed for murdering his brother? And was it by Ham marrying her, and she being saved from the flood in the ark, that "the race which preserved the curse in the land" was perpetuated? If so, then I believe that race is the one through which it is ordained those spirits that were not valiant in the great rebellion in heaven should come; who, through their indifference or lack of integrity to righteousness, rendered themselves unworthy of the Priesthood and its powers, and hence it is withheld from them to this day. (Contributor 6:26-297.)

George A. Smith

George A. Smith, grandfather of the Prophet George Albert Smith and an apostle, stated, "When Cain brought a curse upon his own head and that of his household, his after generations bear the curse. The curse that came upon Canaan, the son of Ham, was extended to a great portion of the human race, and has continued to the present day." (*Journal of Discourses*, 3:29.)

Joseph F. Smith

Joseph F. Smith, later president of the Church, com-

mented on the Negro and the Priesthood in the following
article published in 1924, in the *Improvement Era:*

> The question arises from time to time in regard to the
> Negro race and the Priesthood . . . It is true that the Negro
> race is barred from holding the Priesthood, and this has
> always been the case. The Prophet Joseph Smith taught this
> doctrine. . .

> President Brigham Young, in a discourse given in 1855,
> speaking of the Negro said the following:

>> "It is their privilege to live so as to enjoy many of
>> the blessings which attend obedience to the first prin-
>> ciples of the gospel, though they are not entitled to the
>> Priesthood." *Journal of Discourses* 2:184.

> That one-third of the host of heaven remained neutral
> and therefore were cursed by having a black skin, could
> hardly be true, for the Negro race has not constituted one-
> third of the inhabitants of the earth.

> It is a reasonable thing to believe that the spirits of the
> premortal state were of varying degrees of intelligence and
> faithfulness. This thought is conveyed in many passages of
> scripture such as Acts 17:24-27; Deut. 32:8; Abraham 3:19-
> 26. . . . Therefore, let it suffice that the Negro is barred
> from the Priesthood. . ." (Joseph F. Smith, "The Negro and
> the Priesthood," *Improvement Era*, Vol. 27, 1923-24, pp.
> 564-565.)

The First Presidency—1947

The First Presidency, in answer to a letter written by
Dr. Lowry Nelson, one time head of the Department of
Sociology at BYU, made the following statement:

> We might make this initial remark: The social side of
> the Restored Gospel is only an incident of it; it is not the
> end thereof.

> The basic element of your ideas and concepts seems to
> be that all God's children stand in equal positions before
> Him in all things.

> Your knowledge of the Gospel will indicate to you that
> this is contrary to the very fundamentals of God's dealing
> with Israel dating from the time of His promise to Abra-
> ham regarding Abraham's seed and their position *vis-a-vis*

with God Himself. Indeed, some of God's children were assigned to superior positions before the world was formed. We are aware that some higher critics do not accept this, but the Church does.

Your position seems to lose sight of the revelations of the Lord touching the pre-existence of our spirits, the rebellion in heaven, and the doctrine that our birth into this life and the advantages under which we may be born, have a relationship in the life heretofore.

From the days of the Prophet Joseph even until now, it has been the doctrine of the Church, never questioned by any of the Church leaders, that the Negroes are not entitled to the full blessings of the Gospel.

Furthermore, your ideas, as we understand them, appear to contemplate the intermarriage of the Negro and white races, a concept which has heretofore been most repugnant to most normal-minded people from the ancient patriarchs till now. God's rule for Israel, his Chosen People, has been endogamous. Modern Israel has been similarly directed.

We are not unmindful of the fact that there is a growing tendency, particularly among some educators, as it manifests itself in this area, toward the breaking down of race barriers in the matter of intermarriage between whites and blacks, but it does not have the sanction of the Church and is contrary to Church doctrine. (John J. Stewart, *Mormonism and the Negro*, pp. 46-47.)

The First Presidency—1951

On August 17, 1951, the First Presidency made available an official statement on the Negro question:

The attitude of the Church with reference to Negroes remains as it has always stood. It is not a matter of the declaration of a policy but of direct commandment from the Lord, on which is founded the doctrine of the Church from the days of its organization, to the effect that Negroes may become members of the Church but that they are not entitled to the Priesthood at the present time. The prophets of the Lord have made several statements as to the operation of the principle. President Brigham Young said: "Why are so many of the inhabitants of the earth cursed with a skin of blackness? It comes in consequence of their fathers' rejecting the power of the Holy Priesthood, and the law of God. They will go down to death. And when all the rest of the children have received their blessings in the Holy Priesthood, then that curse will be removed from the seed of Cain, and they will then come up and possess the Priesthood, and receive all the blessings which we now are entitled to."

President Wilford Woodruff made the following statement: "The day will come when all that race will be redeemed and possess all the blessings which we now have."

The position of the Church regarding the Negro may be understood when another doctrine of the Church is kept in mind, namely, that the conduct of spirits in the pre-mortal existence has some determining effect upon the conditions and circumstances under which these spirits take on mortality, and that while the details of this principle have not been made known, the principle itself indicates that the coming to this earth and taking on mortality is a privilege that is given to those who maintained their first estate; and that the worth of the privilege is so great that spirits are willing to come to earth and take on bodies no matter what the handicap may be as to the kind of bodies they are to secure; and that among the handicaps, failure of the right to enjoy in mortality the blessings of the Priesthood, is a handicap which spirits are willing to assume in order that they might come to earth. Under this principle there is no injustice whatsoever involved in this deprivation as to the holding of the Priesthood by the Negroes.

Why the Negro was denied the Priesthood from the days of Adam to our day is not known. The few known facts about our pre-earth life and our entrance into mortality must be taken into account in any attempt at an explanation.

1.   Not all . . . reached the same degree of attainment in the pre-earth life. . . .

2.   Man will be punished for his own sins and not for Adam's transgression. (Second Article of Faith.) If this is carried further, it would imply that the Negro is punished or allotted to a certain position on this earth, not because of Cain's transgression, but came to earth through the loins of Cain because of his failure to achieve other stature in the spirit world.

3. All spirits are born innocent into this world. *Every spirit of man was innocent in the beginning; and God having redeemed man from the fall, men became again, in their infant state, innocent before God.* (D&C 93:38.)

4. The Negro was a follower of Jehovah in the pre-earth life. (There were no neutrals.)

(Berrett, "The Church and the Negroid People," *Mormonism and the Negro*, pp. 16-18.)

David O. McKay

In a letter dated November 3, 1947, President David O. McKay talked about the Negroes and the Priesthood.

Dear Brother:

In your letter to me of October 28, 1947, you say that you and some of your fellow students "have been perturbed about the question of why the Negroid race cannot hold the priesthood."

In reply, I send you the following thoughts that I expressed to a friend upon the same subject:

Stated briefly your problem is simply this:

Since, as Paul states, the Lord "hath made of one blood all nations of men for to dwell on all the face of the earth," why is there shown in the Church of Christ discrimination against the colored race?

This is a perplexing question, particularly in the light of the present trend of civilization to grant equality to all men irrespective of race, creed, or color. The answer, as I have sought it, cannot be found in abstract reasoning, for, in this case, reason to the soul is "dim as the borrowed rays of moon and stars to lonely, weary, wandering travelers."

I know of no scriptural basis for denying the Priesthood to Negroes other than one verse in the Book of Abraham (1:26); however, I believe, as you suggest, that the real reason dates back to our pre-existent life.

This means that the true answer to your question (and it is the only one that has ever given me satisfaction) has its foundation in faith—(1) Faith in a God of Justice, (2) Faith in the existence of an eternal plan of salvation for all God's children.

Faith in a God of Justice Essential

I say faith in a God of *Justice*, because if we hold the Lord responsible for the conditions of the Negro in his relationship to the Church, we must acknowledge justice as an attribute of the Eternal, or conceive Him as a discriminator and therefore unworthy of our worship. In seeking our answer, then, to the problem wherein discrimination seems apparent, we must accept the Lord as being upright, and that "Justice and judgment are the habitation of His throne." (Psalm 89:14), and we must believe that He will "render to every man according to his work," and that He "shall bring every work into judgment, with every secret thing, whether it be good, or whether it be evil." (Eccl. 12-14) Accepting the truth that God is just and righteous, we may then set our minds at rest in the assurance that "Whatsoever good thing any man doeth the same shall be received of the Lord, whether he be bond or free." (Eph. 6:8.)

I emphasize *Justice* as an attribute of Deity, because it is the Lord who, though He "made of one blood all nations," also "determined the bounds of their habitation." In other words, the seeming discrimination by the Church toward the Negro is not something which originated with man, but goes back into the beginning with God.

It was the Lord who said that Pharaoh, the first Governor of Egypt, though "a righteoud man, blessed with the blessings of the earth, with the blessings of wisdom . . . could not have the Priesthood."

Now if we have faith in the justice of God, we are forced to the conclusion that this denial was not a deprivation of merited right. It may have been entirely in keeping with the eternal plan of salvation for all of the children of God.

The Peopling of the Earth is in Accordance with a Great Plan

Revelation assures us that this plan antedates man's mortal existence, extending back to man's pre-existent state. In that pre-mortal state were "intelligences that were organized before the world was; and among all these there were many of the noble and great ones;

"And God saw these souls that they were good, and he stood in the midst of them, and he said: "These I will make my rulers; for he stood among those that were spirits, and he saw that they were good."

Manifestly, from this revelation, we may infer two things: first that there were many among those spirits different degrees of intelligence, varying grades of achievement, retarded and advanced spiritual attainment; second, that there were no national distinctions among those spirits such as Americans, Europeans, Asiatics, Australians, etc. Such "bounds of habitation" would have to be "determined" when the spirits entered upon their earthly existence or second estate.

In the "Blue Bird" Materlinck pictures unborn children summoned to earth life. As one group approaches the earth, the voices of the children earthward tending are heard in the distance to cry: "The earth! the earth! I can see it; how beautiful it is! How bright it is!" Then following these cries of ecstacy there issued from out of the depth of the abyss a sweet song of gentleness and expectancy, in reference to which the author says: "It is the song of the mothers coming out to meet them."

Materlinck's fairy play is not all fantasy or imagination, neither is Wordsworth's "Ode on Intimations of Immortality" wherein he says:

> Our birth is but a sleep and a forgetting,
> The Soul that rises with us, our life's Star,
> Hath had elsewhere its setting
> And cometh from afar;
> Not in entire forgetfulness,
> And not in utter nakedness
> But trailing clouds of glory do we come
> From God, who is our home;

For, as we have already quoted, it is given as a fact in revelation that Abraham was chosen before he was born. Songs of expectant parents come from all parts of the earth, and each little spirit is attracted to the spiritual and mortal parentage for which the spirit had prepared itself.

Now if none of these spirits was permitted to enter mortality until they all were good and great and had become leaders, then the diversity of conditions among the children of men as we see them today would certainly seem to indicate discrimination and injustice. But if in their eagerness to take upon themselves bodies, the spirits were willing to come through any lineage for which they were worthy, or to which they were attracted, then they were given *the full reward of merit, and were satisfied,* yes, and even blessed.

Accepting this theory of life, we have a reasonable explanation of existent conditions in the habitations of man. How the law of spiritual attraction works between the spirit and the expectant parents, has not been revealed, neither can finite mind fully understand. By analogy, however, we can perhaps get a glimpse of what might take place in that spirit world. In physics we refer to the law of attraction wherein some force acting mutually between particles of matter tends to draw them together and to keep them from separating. In chemistry, there is an attractive force exerted between atoms, which causes them to enter into combination. We know, too, that there is an affinity between persons—a spiritual relationship or attraction wherein individuals are either drawn towards others or repelled by others. Might it not be so in the realm of spirit—each individual attracted to the parentage for which it is prepared? Our place in this world would then be determined by our advancement or conditions in the pre-mortal state, just as our place in our future existence will be determined by what we do here in mortality.

When, therefore, the Creator said to Abraham, and to others of his attainment "You I will make my rulers," there could exist no feeling of envy or of jealousy among the million other spirits, for those who were "good and great" were but receiving their just reward, just as do members of a graduation class who have successfully completed their prescribed courses of study. The thousands of other students who have not yet attained that honor still have the privilege to seek it, or they may, if they choose, remain in satisfaction down in the grades.

By the operation of some eternal law with which man is yet unfamiliar, spirits come through parentages for which they are worthy—some as Bushmen of Australia, some as Solomon Islanders, some as Americans, as Europeans, as Asiatics, etc., etc., with all the varying degrees of mentality and spirituality manifest in parents of the different races that inhabit the earth.

Of this we may be sure, each was satisfied and happy to

come through the lineage to which he or she was attracted and for which, and only which, he or she was prepared.

The Priesthood was given to those who were chosen as leaders. There were many who could not receive it, yet who knew that it was possible for them at sometime in the eternal plan to achieve that honor. Even those who knew that they would not be prepared to receive it during their mortal existence were content in the realization that they could attain every earthly blessing—progress intellectually and spiritually, and possess to a limited degree the blessing of wisdom.

George Washington Carver was one of the noblest souls that ever came to earth. He held a close kinship with his Heavenly Father, and rendered a service to his fellow men such as few have ever excelled. For every righteous endeavor, for every noble impulse, for every good deed performed in his useful life, George Washington Carver will be rewarded, and so will every other man be he red, white, black or yellow, for God is no respecter of persons.

Sometime in God's eternal plan, the Negro will be given the right to hold the Priesthood. In the meantime, those of that race who receive the testimony of the Restored Gospel may have their family ties protected and other blessings made secure, for in the justice and mercy of the Lord they will possess all the blessings to which they are entitled in the eternal plan of Salvation and Exaltation.

Nephi 26:33, to which you refer, does not contradict what I have said above, because the Negro is entitled to come unto the Lord by baptism, confirmation, and to receive the assistance of the Church in living righteously.

Sincerely yours,

Signed by David O. McKay.

(Berrett, "The Church and the Negroid People," *Mormonism and the Negro*, pp. 18-23; this letter can also be found in Llewelyn R. McKay's *Home Memories of President David O. McKay*, pp. 226-231.)

Joseph Fielding Smith

Joseph Fielding Smith has had much to say on the Negro question. In addition to those statements cited previously he has made the following remarks:

It is true that the Pearl of Great Price accounts for the lineage of Egyptus, and that the Doctrine and Covenants declares that the spirits of ALL men were innocent *in the beginning*. It also teaches us that following the beginning, and even in the world of spirits there came a rebellion, and that one-third of the hosts of heaven rebelled because of their agency and had to be cast out.

When they were cast out, there were many who did not join the rebellious forces, but who were not valiant. Because of their lack of obedience, they were not deprived of receiving bodies, but came here under restrictions. One of those restrictions is that they were denied the Priesthood. They may come into the Church, but they are not privileged to obtain the Priesthood in this life. They can be baptized, and if faithful to the end, then in the next existence and in the due time of the Lord the restrictions placed upon them in the first existence will be removed. If they do not repent then these restrictions will not be removed.

Children are Born in Innocence

Now the Lord has informed us that when a child is born, it comes in this world innocent. That is to say that it is not subject to any penalty that has to be cleansed such as is taught in the Catholic and most Protestant churches. So far as we are concerned, that child is innocent. It was innocent in the beginning. It is innocent *here* and not to be punished, for as far as mortality is concerned it has committed no sin. Therefore, Negro babies like all other babies are innocent in their "infant state." Should they die, they will be entitled to go to the Celestial Kingdom, just like other babies, because in this life they have done no wrong. (Joseph Fielding Smith, *Answers to Gospel Questions*, 5:163-64.)

Another averment he made about the Negro was, "Millions of souls have come into this world cursed with a black skin and have been denied the privilege of Priesthood and the fulness of the blessings of the Gospel. These are the descendants of Cain." (Joseph Fielding Smith, *The Way to Perfection*, p. 101.)

Alvin R. Dyer

. . . you often may have heard, missionaries say it or have asked the question: Why is a Negro a Negro? And, you have heard this answer. Well, they must have been neutral in the pre-existence or they must have straddled the fence. That is the most common saying—they were neither hot nor cold, so the Lord made them Negroes. This, of course, is not true. The reason that spirits are born into Negro bodies is *because those spirits rejected the Priesthood of God in the pre-existence.* This is the reason why you have Negroes upon the earth.

You will observe that when Cain was influenced by the power of Lucifer to follow him and to fall down and worship him in the beginning, it was then that the Lord came to him and said, Cain, if you will abide the law—if you will keep the commandments, you too can be acceptable unto me. But Cain rejected the counsel of God. He rejected again the Priesthood as his forebears had done in the pre-existence. Therefore, the curse of the pre-existence was made institute through the loins of Cain. Consequently, you have then the beginning of the race of men and women into which would be born those in the pre-existence who had rejected the Priesthood of God. . . . Ham reinstated the curse of the pre-existence when he rejected the Priesthood of Noah. He rejected the Priesthood of Noah, and in consequence of that, he preserved the curse in the earth. Therefore, the Negroes to be born thereafter, or those who were to become Negroes were to be born through the loins of Ham. . . .

. . . in the early days when the Egyptian government was established under its first rulers, the pharaohs, they set up a system that was exactly like the Priesthood of God. It was exactly like the Patriarchal order, but they said knowing that they could not have the birthright, they thought to capitalize on the form or the order of administration. *The Pearl of Great Price* tells us specifically that they knew that they could not hold the Priesthood, yet they used the same type of organization. . . . (Alvin R. Dyer, "For What Purpose," a talk given to the Norwegian Mission, May 1961, taken from book by R. M. Frame, *The Negro Question,* May 1964.)

Melvin J. Ballard

Now, my brothers and sisters, I would like you to understand that long before we were born into this earth we were tested and tried in our pre-existence. Of the thousands of children born today, a certain proportion of them went to Hottentots of South Africa; thousands went to Chinese mothers; thousands went to Negro mothers; thousands to beautiful white Latter-day Saint mothers. Now you cannot tell me that all these spirits were just arbitrarily designated, marked, to go where they did, that they were men and women of equal opportunities. There are no infant spirits born. They had a being ages before they came into this life. They appear in infant bodies, but they were tested, proven souls. Therefore, I say to you that long before we came into this life all groups and races of men existed as they exist today. Like attracts like.

Why is it in this Church we do not grant the Priesthood to the Negroes? It is alleged that the Prophet Joseph said—and I have no reason to dispute it—that it is because of some act committed by them before they came into this life. I am convinced it is because of some things they did before they came into this life that they have been denied the privilege. The races of today are very largely reaping the consequences of a previous life. (Melvin R. Ballard, *Melvin J. Ballard—Crusader for Righteousness,* p. 218.)

Hugh B. Brown

Hugh B. Brown, in a semi-annual conference speech given October 6, 1963, in Salt Lake City, gave the following remarks:

During recent months, both in Salt Lake City and across the nation, considerable interest has been expressed in the position of The Church of Jesus Christ of Latter-day Saints on the matter of civil rights. We would like it to be known that there is in this Church no doctrine, belief, or practice that is intended to deny the enjoyment of full civil rights by any person regardless of race, color, or creed. We call upon all men, everywhere, both within and outside the Church, to commit themselves to the establishment of full civil equality for all of God's children. Anything less defeats our high ideals of the brotherhood of man.

We say again, as we have said many times before, that we believe that all men are the children of the same God, and that it is a moral evil for any person or group of persons to deny any human being the right to gainful employment, to full educational opportunity, and to every privilege of citizenship, just as it is a moral evil to deny him the right to worship according to the dictates of his own conscience.

We have consistently and persistently upheld the Constitution of the United States, and as far as we are concerned, this means upholding the constitutional right of every citizen of the United States. (*The Improvement Era*, December 1963, p. 1058.)

X

QUESTIONS AND ANSWERS
ABOUT THE NEGRO AND MORMONISM

IT HAS BEEN THE PRIVILEGE OF THIS AUTHOR TO TRAVEL extensively lecturing at various meetings and firesides on the Negro question. During these travels it was noticed that certain questions were asked with greater frequency than others. It is the purpose of this section to answer in a most concise manner those questions that were most commonly asked.

Question: Was Cain the first child of Adam and Eve?

Answer: No. There were many children born to Adam and Eve prior to the birth of Cain. It is true that Cain was the first child mentioned by name in the *King James Version* of the Bible. This does not say, however, that he was the first child. In the *Inspired Version* as well as the *Pearl of Great Price* we are told that Adam and Eve were grandparents before Cain was born. (See Gen. 4:2, 3, 12, 13, *Inspired Version of the Bible;* see also Moses 5:2, 3, 12, 13, *Pearl of Great Price.*

Question: Was Cain foreordained to do evil?

Answer: No, Cain was not foreordained to do evil. The Lord said He would accept him if he did well, thus indicating that Cain did not have to do evil. (See Gen. 4:7, King James.) All are given their free agency in this existence and may choose either the good or the evil as they so desire. No one is foreordained to do evil. God only foreordains men to do good. (See Joseph Fielding Smith, *Answers to Gospel Questions,* II:193-94; see also Jer. 1:5, King James.)

Question: Did Abraham, Joseph, and Moses marry Negro women when they were in Egypt?

Answer: For the answer to this question we go to an explanation by Joseph Fielding Smith:

If Abraham, Joseph, and Moses had married Negro wives their descendants would have been denied the Priesthood according to the word of the Lord to Abraham. (Abraham 1:21-27.) Had such a thing happened the Lord would not have called Israel as a chosen people, neither would he have chosen the Prophet Joseph Smith and given him the keys of authority for the Dispensation of the Fulness of Times, as he was a descendant of Joseph and of Abraham.

For many years preceding the time of Abraham the descendants of Egyptus occupied and governed in Egypt. They extended their dominion into the land of Canaan and oppressed the people, but the time came when the people of Asia, who were of the Semitic race, rebelled and made war on the Egyptians and conquered the country, driving the original inhabitants farther south and up the Nile. These Semitic people known as Hyksos, or shepherds, for they had many flocks and herds, were in possession of the land of Egypt for many years before the time of Abraham. Their rule lasted for some five hundred years, and they were in possession of the land when Joseph was taken into Egypt. It was a Hyksos king who befriended Joseph and who was friendly with Abraham and Isaac. While these people occupied the land of Egypt, they were called Egyptians, although they were relatives of Abraham and Joseph, being descendants of Shem . . .

So Abraham, Joseph, and Moses married women of their own race, and we need have no worry over our lineage, because we are of that same race. (Joseph Fielding Smith, *Answers to Gospel Questions*, 1:169-71.)

Question: Why can those of other races who have a darker skin than some Negroes hold the Priesthood?

Answer: The reason for not allowing the Negro to hold the Priesthood is not due to skin color. A dark skin in the case of the Negro may or may not accompany the curse. The issue is not one of skin color but of Priesthood. It will be remembered that Cain was selected to be the father of all those who were to come to earth and not possess the Priesthood. There were no exceptions. Therefore, no one who is a descendant of Cain, regardless of whether he is black, brown, red, yellow, or white is allowed to hold the Priesthood. (See Matthew Cowley's *Wilford Woodruff,* p. 351.)

The mark of a dark skin in the case of other races is symbolic of a different loss of blessings. It is possible therefore for a person with a darker skin than some Negroes to hold the Priesthood.

Question: Why do people have dark colored skin?

Answer: Undoubtedly a medical student would say that skin color or pigment is the result of a material known as melanin. The greater the amount of melanin the darker the pigmentation or color of the skin. This does not tell, however, why some have more melanin than others. The old "out in the sun theory" is generally disregarded as an acceptable explanation. One may simply point out the example of the Eskimo whose entire body is covered, with the exception of the face, from birth until death. Yet, the Eskimo has a dark skin all over his body. If the sun theory were valid, then generations of Eskimos should produce a lighter skin color; but, it hasn't.

The scriptures relate several reasons for skin color. One of the most important will be mentioned here:

> And he had caused the cursing to come upon them, yea, even a sore cursing, because of their iniquity. For behold, they had hardened their hearts against him, that they had become like unto a flint; wherefore, as they were white, and exceeding fair and delightsome, that they might not be enticing unto my people the Lord God did cause a skin of blackness to come upon them.
>
> And thus saith the Lord God: I will cause that they shall be loathsome unto thy people, save they shall repent of their iniquities.
>
> And cursed shall be the seed of him that mixeth with their seed; for they shall be cursed even with the same cursing. And the Lord spake it, and it was done. (II Nephi 5:21-23, *The Book of Mormon.*)

When people rebel against God's commandments, either during their pre-earth life or while in mortality, they are given a dark skin so that those who are of the chosen seed will not inter-marry with them.

Another reason for a dark skin was given in the story of Cain. A dark skin was placed on Cain as a sign of protection lest any finding him should kill him. The mark of a dark skin was placed on Cain's descendants for an entirely different reason. They were marked because of the Priesthood curse they had acquired in the pre-mortal life.

Question: Is it seven times worse to kill a Negro than it is to kill a member of another race?

Answer: No. Murder is murder regardless of the murdered or the murderer. The false notion of it being seven times worse to harm a Negro probably had its origin in the Lord's words to Cain: "Whosoever slayeth Cain vegeance shall be taken on him sevenfold." (See Gen. 4:15, King James.) It should be noted that this pronouncement applied to Cain only. A man who purposefully sheds innocent blood may rest assured that he has broken the commandments of God and will suffer the punishments that God has prepared for murderers.

Question: Were Negroes neutral in the great war in heaven (Rev. 12:7) and therefore denied the Priesthood during mortality?

Answer: No. There were no neutrals in the war in heaven. An individual was either on the side of Christ or the side of Lucifer. John reveals that one-third of the "stars of heaven" or the children of God followed Satan and were cast out of heaven. (Rev. 12:4.) The Negroes were not neutral; they were sufficiently valiant to be promised the Priesthood, if worthy, after their mortal existence. (See Joseph Fielding Smith, *Doctrines of Salvation,* compiled by Bruce R. McConkie, 1:65-66.)

Question: Can a man who holds the Melchizedek Priesthood be sealed (married) in an LDS Temple to a Negress?

Answer: No. Temple endowments and sealings are blessings of the Priesthood and it is not yet time for the Negroes to receive these blessings. It is not enough that the man hold the Melchizedek Priesthood in order to be married in the Temple. His spouse must also be able to bear children who are entitled to the Priesthood. If a man were to marry a Negress they would not be able to have children who could possess the Priesthood. (Joseph Fielding Smith, *Answers to Gospel Questions*, 5:168.

Question: The Church "gave in" on polygamy; why doesn't it "give in" on the Negro question?

Answer: There are those both in and out of the Church who believe that the doctrine and practice of polygamy were ended because of social and governmental pressure that was brought to bear on the Church. Some of these same people reason that in order for the Mormon Church to give the Negro the Priesthood it will again be necessary to use social and political pressure. Those who believe that the Church "gave in" on the polygamy issue and subsequently should give in on the Negro question are not only misinformed about Church History, but are apparently unaware of Church doctrine.

CHURCH HISTORY: A close examination of Church History will reveal that the Church did not "give in" on the polygamy issue. Anyone vaguely familiar with Mormon history will recall that the Church has constantly been under social and/or political pressure. It will be remembered that the members left four states (i.e. New York, Ohio, Missouri, Illinois) in order to practice their religious beliefs and live as they felt God wanted them to live. One exodus took them out of the United States to a desert wilderness which became known as Utah. Colonies were established in many areas, including Mexico and Canada. Is there any doubt that the Mormons would have "packed up" and moved out rather than violate a commandment which came from God? It is entirely possible that headquarters could be in Mexico or Canada today had not the Lord given a revelation to Wilford Woodruff to cease, for the time being, the practice of polygamy.

CHURCH DOCTRINE: It is the Church's stand that changes in doctrine come only through revelation from the Lord to the Prophet. Wilford Woodruff said concerning the manifesto in the *Doctrine and Covenants* (pp. 256-57), "I want to say to all Israel that the step which I have taken in issuing this manifesto has not been done without earnest prayer before the Lord. I am about to go to the spirit world . . . and for me to have taken a stand on anything which is not pleasing in the sight of God, or before the heavens, I would rather have gone out and been shot." (Matthew Cowley, *Wilford woodruff,* pp. 570-71.)

The above statement by Wilford Woodruff would certainly indicate that he did not fear social pressure or government sanctions. He was ready to meet death rather than "give in." This is also true in the case of the Negro and the Priesthood. It is not a matter of "giving in" but a matter of revelation from God. Therefore, those who hope that pressure will bring about a revelation need to take a closer look at Mormon history and the order of heaven.

XI

SUMMARY

U NRIGHTEOUS DISCRIMINATION IS A SOCIAL EVIL WHICH
is condemned by the Church. The admonition of
the Savior to treat others as one would want to be treated
himself is still the standard of The Church of Jesus Christ
of Latter-day Saints. It is admitted that all Mormons are
not perfect and therefore one may find in the Church
those who discriminate. However, the charge of discrimination should be laid at the feet of that individual, not at
his church.

The phrase "all men are created equal" is questionable
in the areas of social, economic or intellectual capacities,
but it is certainly unquestioned that before God all are
born innocent into this mortal existence. One might challenge whether everyone is treated equal before the laws of
men. Without doubt, however, all men are equal before
the laws of God in that each will be held accountable for
the use of the light and knowledge that he has received.

The mark of Cain, as indicated by Biblical scholars
and confirmed by Latter-day Saint Church leaders and the
Standard Works, was a black skin for Cain and his posteri-
ity. This distinquishing characteristic served several purposes. It marked Cain as the Father of the Negroid race.
It also acted as a sign of protection for Cain and set his
seed apart from the rest of Adam's children so there would
be no intermarriage.

Some have believed that the mark and the curse of
Cain were one and the same. The mark of a dark skin was
separate from the curse although generally the two are
found together. It is possible to have a light-colored skin
and still carry the curse of no Priesthood.

The curse of Cain was that of a Son of Perdition with
its subsequent loss of Priesthood blessings. He brought this

damnation upon himself by misusing the Priesthood that he held. He also rejected all that was connected with God and chose to follow the ways of wickedness. Shortly after cursing Cain, the Lord pronounced a sevenfold vengeance upon anyone that might slay him. It was the Lord's decision to send those spirits who proved themselves unworthy of the Priesthood in the pre-existence through the lineage of Cain.

A close examination of the Cain and Abel story reveals the reasons for the Lord's rejection of Cain. A major consideration was the murder of Abel but this was not the sole criterion for his rejection. He was guilty of a far greater crime. Cain committed the sin against the Holy Ghost, known also as the unpardonable sin, of which there is no forgiveness in this world or the next. This most grievous sin not only consisted of rejecting God's plan for the salvation of man, but also of fighting against that plan.

Cain's rebelliousness and Abel's righteousness were exemplified in the offerings that each made. Abel brought forth what the Lord had required, an animal sacrifice symbolic of the Atonement of Jesus Christ. The shedding of an animal's blood was a foreshadow of the Redeemer's sacrifice on Calvary. Cain likewise made an offering; but it was unacceptable for two reasons. In the first place, Cain's motive for obeying the Lord was not a righteous one. Satan commanded him to do it. Secondly, Cain's offering of the fruits of the ground was a rejection of the Atonement of Jesus Christ, which fact Cain knew well.

Typical of Cain's rebellious spirit, was the slaying of his brother Abel. This abominable act was not a crime of passion as some have supposed, but a case of cold-blooded and calculated murder. The plot against Abel had its foundation in a covenant that Lucifer made with Cain. Satan promised to be subject to Cain in the eternities if he would slay Abel. The motives for this deed were founded in the hope of destroying God's plan of redeeming His children. It can be supposed that Cain and Satan expected that the killing of Abel would thwart the plan of God. One will recall that Abel held the birthright of the

Holy Priesthood because of the unworthiness of the rest of Adam's sons. It was through this chosen birthright seed that the Savior of the world was to come. By killing Abel and preventing him from having any offspring, Cain and Satan perhaps thought they would prevent the Savior from coming to earth and making His atoning sacrifice. Had their plan been successful, all who came to this earth would have become subject to Cain and to the Devil in the eternities. Without the Atonement of Jesus Christ there would have been no resurrection from the dead, forgiveness of sin, or conquering of Hell. Thus, all would remain "filthy still" and since no unclean thing can enter into the presence of God, all would be shut out from God's kingdom and subsequently be subject to Satan's rule. The Lord, however, sent Seth to the earth, who was a righteous son of Adam, worthy of the birthright of the Priesthood. Seth replaced Abel and became a father of the chosen seed, thus frustrating Cain and Satan's attempt to destroy the plan of God.

Cain was also the father of a specific lineage; but, his descendants were those who were not allowed to have the Priesthood during their mortal existence due to their pre-mortal behavior. His offspring have continued in abundance and are found on the earth today. The seed of Cain were preserved through the flood when Ham, a son of Noah, married Egyptus, a descendant of Cain.

In studying the story of Cain, one should remember that Cain could have been exalted to the highest throne in the Celestial Kingdom. God had promised him, "If thou doest well thou shalt be accepted." Cain, of his own free will, chose not to do well; he chose to love Satan more than God and will suffer the consequences of his rebellious behavior.

It is true that all Negroes are descendants of Cain and are not entitled to the Priesthood. The denial of Priesthood, however, is not related in any way to the sins of Cain. The Priesthood, which is the authority to act in the name of God in performing ordinances of the Gospel, is denied to the Negroes because of their behavior in the pre-mortal existence. Before coming to earth all were brothers and sisters, all were sons and daughters of God. There was a judgment in this pre-earth life just as there will be a judgment at the end of earth life. Each individual was judged according to his faith, talents and individual worthiness. Each was assigned to come to earth in a particular race, time and nation commensurate with their works and use of their free agency in the pre-mortal sphere. In other words, all those who are descendants of Cain have been restricted concerning the Priesthood because they were unworthy in the pre-existence.

The curse of no Priesthood for Cain was totally different from the curse of no Priesthood for the Negroes, who are the descendants of Cain. Negroes are kept from holding the Priesthood because of something they did before they came to earth; Cain was damned because of something he did while on the earth. Cain's sin against the Holy Ghost brought upon him a permanent curse of no Priesthood. It is written and prophesied, however, that the curse of no Priesthood for his descendants is not a permanent one. The Negroes will receive the Priesthood in the next life if they prove worthy during their mortal existence.

There is then a proper time for the Negroes to receive the Priesthood. It should be emphasized, however, that they must use this mortal existence to prove their faithfulness. Those who would try to pressure the Prophet to give the Negroes the Priesthood do not understand the plan of God nor the order of heaven. Revelation is the expressed will of God to man. Revelation is not man's will expressed to God. All the social, political, and governmental pressure in the world is not going to change what God has decreed to be.

There are two time stipulations that will have to be met before the Negroes will be allowed to possess the Priesthood, even if they are worthy. (This is similar to a boy who is worthy at age eleven to hold the Priesthood but does not receive it until age twelve.) First, all of Adam's children will have to resurrect and secondly, the seed of

Abel must first have an opportunity to possess the Priesthood. These events will not occur until sometime after the end of the millennium. It would be unwise to say that Negroes will receive the Priesthood during their mortal existence. Again it should be emphasized that the Negroes are not made to wait this long time to hold the Priesthood because of Cain's transgression, but because of their own acts in the pre-existence. The holding of Priesthood is dependent upon individual worthiness, and the Negro who is worthy during this life will no doubt hold the Priesthood in the next life while many who now hold the Priesthood, but do not honor it, will lose their Priesthood blessings.

Interracial marriage with the Negro is forbidden. Those who are allowed to have the Priesthood during their mortal life should not intermarry with those who are not allowed to have it. Marriage between the two would result in children coming to that marriage who would not be entitled to the Priesthood.

The Mormon Church can offer the Negro more than any other religious organization. A Negro may be baptized and confirmed a member of The Church of Jesus Christ of Latter-day Saints. He may be called to serve as a teacher in any of the auxiliary organizations of the Church. He may also be called to be an administrator in the Sunday School, Mutual Improvement Association, Primary, or Relief Society. As a member of the Church, a worthy Negro is expected to pray, partake of the Sacrament and bear testimony of Christ. He may receive a Patriarchal blessing, enter the temple to be baptized for the dead, serve as a missionary and sustain the officers of the Church. He should pay one-tenth of all he earns to the Church, fast, and not partake of foods or beverages that would adversly affect his body such as alcoholic drinks, coffe, tea, cigarettes, or tobacco in any form. He is also expected to live a clean moral life free from any improper sex relationships. When he marries, he is expected to raise his children according to the commandments of Christ.

There are Negroes now, as there have been since the early days of LDS history, who are members of the Church. Many are highly respected because of the noble lives they lead. Many have given testimony to the divine origin of the Mormon Church and to the mission of the Prophet Joseph Smith.

The Church leaders from the earliest times up to and including the present have never changed their position concerning the Negro. Simply stated, no one who is a descendant of Cain may function in any capacity requiring Priesthood. Negroes, however, are entitled to all other blessings of the Gospel and should not be treated with any less respect than one would treat Jesus Christ if He were to come into one's own home.

XII

ANNOTATED BIBLIOGRAPHY

Following is a partial list of references of Cain and the Negro. Some of these have been previously cited in this book. An effort was made, however, to avoid needless duplication. A researcher may find these additional quotes valuable in gathering further information on this subject.

The Book of Mormon:
    Negro:
        Alma ch. 13   All those who were worthy received the Priesthood in the pre-existence.

Pearl of Great Price:
    Cain:
        Moses 5:16   The birth of Cain
        Moses 5:18   Cain loved Satan more than God.
        Moses 5:18   Satan commanded Cain to make an offering.
        Moses 5:23   Cain will rule over Satan.
        Moses 5:24   Cain was called Perdition from the very beginning.
        Moses 5:28   Cain marries; he and his wife love Satan more than God.
        Moses 5:29   Cain is sworn to secrecy by Satan, thus the beginning of secret oaths and combinations.
        Moses 5:32   Cain slew Abel.
        Moses 5:36   Cain was cursed.
        Moses 5:42   Cain built a city called Enoch.
        Moses 5:43   The genealogy of Cain's descendants to Lamech is given.
        Moses 7:22   The seed of Cain were black.

Negro:

> Abraham 1:20-27 The Pharaoh was of the lineage of Cain and could not hold the Priesthood.

Journal of Discourses:

Cain:

> Vol. 3:29 Elder G. A. Smith: The Lord conferred portions of Priesthood upon certain races of men. Loss of Priesthood, whether in an individual case or that of a race, is a result of wickedness.
>
> Vol. 11:272 Brigham Young: Why are so many of the inhabitants of the earth cursed with a skin of blackness? It is because they rejected the Priesthood. Negroes will not hold the Priesthood until after the resurrection of all of Adam's children.
>
> Vol. 21:370 Erastus Snow: Cain forfeited the Priesthood blessings and the right to the Priesthood because of his unworthiness.
>
> Vol. 22:301 John Taylor: Cain's offering was rejected because of the personal wickedness of Cain. Satan became represented on the earth in the mind and will of Cain and God was likewise represented in Abel.
>
> Vol. 24:349-50 John Taylor: Cain made a compact with Satan; yet, at the same time he wanted to receive the blessings of God. Many are that same way today. They would like the blessings of God but they want the Devil mixed in with it.

Cain harbored a spirit of hatred against God, His laws, and His people.

Vol. 25:48-47   Charles W. Penrose: The offerings that Cain and Abel made were to be symbolic of the coming Redeemer who should come in the meridian of time and pour out his blood for the remission of sins. Cain offered what he pleased and was summarily rejected

Vol. 25:339   Charles W. Penrose: Not just any offering is acceptable in remembrance of the Atonement. Cain was rejected because of an improper offering.

Vol. 26:88-89   John Taylor: Cain was an enemy of all righteousness and rejected the Atonement of Jesus Christ. Cain was not willing that the plan of redemption and salvation, which was devised before this world was, should be carried out. Abel played a very important role in that plan; therefore, Cain killed him. However, another seed was raised up to Adam, namely Seth, to stand in the place of Abel. He took Abel's place as a representative of God on earth.

Negro:

Vol. 2:184-85   Brigham Young: The conduct of the whites toward the Negroes will in many cases send the whites to hell.

Vol. 7:290-91   Cain was the father of the Negroid race and was marked with a black skin. If Cain had been killed it would have terminated this line through Cain. Cain was the first to be cursed and will be the last to be redeemed. The Negroes will come forth in due time and receive the blessings of the Priesthood.

Vol. 10:110-11   Brigham Young: I am no abolitionist, neither am I a pro-slavery man.

The Improvement Era:

Negro:

Conference talk given by Hugh B. Brown, (December, 1963), p. 1058, wherein he comments on civil rights.

"My Responsibility," a testimony by John Lamb, a Negro Mormon, (January, 1966), 36-37.

"The Negro and the Priesthood," a statement by Joseph F. Smith, Vol. 27 (1923-24), pp. 564-65.

Berrett, William E., and Alma P. Burton. *Readings in LDS Church History.* Salt Lake City, Utah: Deseret Book Company, 1953. Vol. I.

Negro:

p. 157   A letter from a mob to the governor of Missouri saying that the people were afraid that the Mormons would bring in free Negroes.

p. 159   A mob threatened to use Negro slaves against the Mormons.

p. 286   The Mormons and the Negroes were the only ones not allowed to vote.

Brooks, Melvin R. *LDS Reference Encyclopedia.* Salt Lake City, Utah: Bookcraft, Inc., 1960.

Cain:

p. 61   Cain was cursed in five ways:
(1) The earth would not yield abundantly for him.

(2) He would be a fugitive and a vagabond in the earth.

(3) A mark was placed on him.

(4) He was shut out from the presence of the Lord.

(5) He lost his rights to the Priesthood.

Negroes:

p. 115   Egyptus was the wife of Ham and one of the daughters of Ham was also named Egyptus. The wife of Ham was a descendant of Cain and must have been a righteous person since only eight righteous souls were saved at the time of the flood.

p. 167   Ham married a Negress and thus the seed of Cain was preserved through the flood. Ham's children were not allowed to have the Priesthood. His sons were Cush, Mizraim, Phut, and Canaan.

pp. 327-28   Negroes may be baptized into the Church. They are not allowed to hold the Priesthood due to some act of their own in the pre-existence.

Carter, Kate B. (comp.), *Our Pioneer Heritage.* 9 vols. Salt Lake City, Utah: Daughters of Utah Pioneers, 1965.

Negro:

Vol. 8:497-580   "The Negro Pioneer in Utah" Bibliographical sketches of early Mormon Negroes.

Clark, James R., Ed. D., *Messages of the First Presidency.* Salt Lake City, Utah: Bookcraft Inc., Vol. I.

Cain:

p. 35   Cain's offering is discussed. Cain

could have no faith in his offering because it was not an animal offering which was symbolic of the Atonement of Jesus Christ. Cain's offering was a rejection of the Atonement.

p. 36   The shedding of blood in an animal offering was symbolic of the remission of sins.

Negro:

p. 51   Even though the Church was not for slavery it did not encourage the slaves to run away from their masters.

pp. 58-59   Missionaries were kept from teaching the Gospel to slaves without their master's consent.

p. 77   The Saints were charged with being dangerous where slavery was tolerated and practiced.

p. 169   The prophecy concerning the starting of the civil war over the slave issue is given.

p. 191   The Prophet Joseph Smith declared that slaves have inalienable rights.

p. 199   The Prophet Joseph encourages that all slaves be bought at a reasonable price and set free.

p. 200   The Prophet seeks freedom for those of all colors, clime, or tongue.

p. 202   Joseph tells of the injustice of slavery.

Clark, J. Reuben, *On the Way to Immortality and Eternal Life.* Deseret Book, 1953.

Cain:

p. 137   Cain was removed because of an unacceptable offering.

Cowley, Matthew F., *Wilford Woodruff*. Salt Lake City, Utah: Bookcraft, 1964.

> Cain:
>
> p. 351   The mark of Cain is on every Negro.

Hunter, Milton R., *Pearl of Great Price Commentary*. Salt Lake City, Utah: Bookcraft, 1951.

> Cain:
>
> p. 140   Cain is called Perdition.
>
> p. 141   The curses of Cain were a dark skin and the loss of the Priesthood.
>
> p. 141   The early leaders of the Church taught the doctrine that the Negroes were the descendants of Cain and could not hold the Priesthood.
>
> p. 142   Joseph Smith taught that the Negroes could not hold the Priesthood or act in any of the offices until the seed of Abel received that Priesthood.

Ludlow, Daniel H. (comp.), *Latter-day Prophets Speak*. Salt Lake City, Utah: Bookcraft, 1951.

> Cain:
>
> p. 204   Brigham Young: The posterity of Cain will receive the Priesthood after all others have had that opportunity.
>
> p. 204   Brigham Young: Any man having one drop of the seed of Cain cannot hold the Priesthood.
>
> Negroes:
>
> p. 205   Brigham Young: The Negroes will eventually receive the Priesthood.

McConkie, Bruce R., *Mormon Doctrine*. Salt Lake City, Utah: Bookcraft, Inc., 1966.

Cain:

Negro:

p. 535	The Priesthood is the power of God to officiate in Gospel ordinances.
p. 553	All men come from common ancestors, Noah and Adam.
p. 554	The posterity of Ham is cursed with Negroid characteristics.
p. 554	The race and nation in which men are born is a result of preexistent life.

Newquist, Jerreld L., *Prophets, Principles and National Survival.*

Negro:

pp. 488-506	This is a general discussion of the Negro issue.

Roberts, B. H., *Comprehensive History of the Church.*

1:327	Slaves were to be considered real estate.
1:302-303	Some believe that the civil war fulfilled the prophecy of the slaves rising up against their masters.
1:334	In 1839, there were less than a dozen Negro members of the Church.
2:192	The Prophet Joseph preaches abolition of slavery.
2:206	The Prophet recommends more equality among the people.
5:8	Buy the slaves and set them free.

Smith, Hyrum M., *Doctrine and Covenants Commentary.*

Cain:

p. 749	Cain was not an honest tithe payer.

Smith, Joseph Fielding, *Answers to Gospel Questions.* 5 vols. Salt Lake City, Utah: Deseret Book Company, 1957-66.

Cain:

2:170-72	Cain is to rule over Satan in the eternities because Cain has a body.
2:173-78	The black skin was not the curse. The curse was the loss of the Priesthood.
4:132	Cain's punishment was worse than had he just been put to death.

Negro:

1:53-55	All children who die are heirs of the Celestial Kingdom, including Negro children.
1:169-71	Abraham, Joseph, and Moses married Egyptian women; but, these women were not Negresses.
2:184-88	Negroes may join the Church, but they are restricted as pertaining to the Priesthood. It is not man that restricts the Negroes from holding the Priesthood, but God.
4:169-72	The Mormon Church can do more for the Negro than all the other churches combined.
5:162-64	The Negroes can be baptized and if faithful they will receive the Priesthood in the next existence in the due time of the Lord. If they do not repent they will not receive the Priesthood.
5:168	Negroes may receive Patriarchal blessings but are not allowed to take out their endowments.

Smith, Joseph Fielding, *Doctrines of Salvation.* 3 vols. (Bruce R. McConkie, comp.), Salt Lake City, Utah: Bookcraft, 1954-56.

Cain:

1:49	Son of Perdition: All who partake of this, the greatest sin, sell themselves as Cain did to Lucifer. They would crucify our Lord again.
1:61	Why are there different races? Some are black and some are white because of pre-existent behavior and judgment.
1:61	Men are not foreordained to evil; Cain would have been accepted had he repented.
2:279	Cain is to rule over Satan in the eternities because Cain has a body.
2:280	Cain sinned with his eyes open and thus became Perdition.

Negro:

1:66	There were no neutrals in Heaven; the Negro is receiving the reward he merits.
2:55	Children who die before they reach the age of accountability are heirs to the Celestial Kingdom. This includes Negro children.
2:55	Negroes have the right to join the Church. There are many Negroes who are members of the Church now.
3:172	"Negroes and Patriarchal Blessings." Negroes may be baptized and receive Patriarchal blessings.

Smith, Joseph Fielding, *Man . . . His Origin and Destiny.* Salt Lake City, Utah: Deseret Book Company, 1954.

Cain:

p. 541	The Sons of Perdition will resur-

rect. Therefore, Cain will resurrect, thus having more power
than Satan.

p. 342   Abel has been resurrected and
holds the keys to his dispensation.

p. 343   If Cain had fulfilled the law of
righteousness he could have
worked with God all the days of
his life.

Smith, Joseph Fielding, *The Way to Perfection*. Eleventh edition. Salt Lake City, Utah: Genealogical Society of The Church of Jesus Christ of Latter-day Saints, 1958.

Cain:

p. 97   Cain was born an heir to an everlasting inheritance in righteous-
ness and he threw it all away.

p. 98   Cain sinned against the light and
this is what made of him a Son
of Perdition. He definitely held
the Priesthood.

p. 103   The curse of Cain was continued
through the flood through the
posterity of Ham.

pp. 106-107   Abel was cut off in his youth
without posterity.

p. 107   A skin of blackness was the mark
of the curse.

p. 110   The seed of Cain cannot receive
the Priesthood or act in any
offices of the Priesthood until the
seed of Abel should come forward
and take precedence over Cain's
offspring.

Negro:

p. 42   We have learned through the
word of the Lord to Abraham that
spirits in the pre-existence were
graded. Some were cast out of

<table>
<tr><td></td><td>heaven altogether, some sent to earth with certain restrictions placed upon them, and some were sent to this earth as a chosen people.</td></tr>
<tr><td>p. 43</td><td>Man had his agency in the pre-existence. The Negroes were there restricted from the Priesthood because of some act of their own.</td></tr>
<tr><td>p. 101</td><td>Millions of souls have come into this world cursed with a black skin and have been denied the privilege of the Priesthood and of the fullness of the blessings of the Gospel. These are the descendants of Cain.</td></tr>
<tr><td>p. 105</td><td>There were no neutrals in heaven. The Negroes and all others were followers of Christ.</td></tr>
</table>

Smith, Joseph Fielding (comp.), *Teachings of the Prophet Joseph Smith.* Salt Lake City, Utah: Deseret Book Company, 1965.

Cain:

<table>
<tr><td>p. 58</td><td>Cain's sacrifice was not accepted because it was an improper sacrifice.</td></tr>
<tr><td>p. 169</td><td>Cain was authorized to offer a sacrifice; he was cursed because of his misuse of the Priesthood.</td></tr>
<tr><td>p. 169</td><td>Abel appeared to Paul as a resurrected person and holds the keys to his dispensation.</td></tr>
</table>

Negro:

<table>
<tr><td>p. 269</td><td>The Negro should be socially equal to any man.</td></tr>
</table>

Smith, Joseph, Jr., *History of the Church.* Salt Lake City, Utah: Deseret Book Company, 1946.

Cain:

2:15   The failure of Cain was due to a lack of faith in the sacrifice he made of the fruits of the ground.

Negro:

1:377-79   The membership of Negroes was discouraged in Missouri.

2:440   The Master's consent was needed before the Gospel could be taught to the slaves.

5:217   The Prophet's views on the Negro race: Change their situation with the whites and Negroes would be like them. Joseph Smith said he would confine the Negroes by strict law to their own race and put them on a national equalization.

Sperry, Sidney B., *Doctrine and Covenants Compendium.* Salt Lake City, Utah: Bookcraft, 1960.

Negro:

p. 236   The Negroes are descendants of Ham.

p. 420   The prophecy about the slaves to rise up against their masters has yet to be fulfilled.

Stewart, John J., *Mormonism and the Negro.* William E. Berrett, "The Church and the Negroid People," (supplement). Second edition, Orem, Utah: Bookmark Division of Community Press Publishing Company, 1960.

Cain and the entire question of the Negro is discussed. Letters and a special declaration on the Negro from the First Presidency are included.

Widtsoe, John A., *Discourses of Brigham Young.*

Cain:

p. 104   Cain conversed with his God every day; he knew all about the plan of salvation, for his father told him.

Negro:

p. 279

The seed of Ham, which is the seed of Cain descending through Ham, because of the curse put upon him, will serve his brethren.

XIII

BIBLIOGRAPHY

Ballard, Melvin R. (comp.). *Melvin J. Ballard—Crusader for Righteousness.* Salt Lake City, Utah: Bookcraft, 1966.

Berrett, William E. "The Church and the Negroid People," Supplement to *Mormonism and the Negro.* John J. Stewart. Second edition. Orem, Utah: Bookmark Division of Community Press Publishing Company, 1960.

Brooks, Melvin R. (comp.). *LDS Reference Encyclopedia.* Salt Lake City, Utah: Bookcraft, Inc., 1960.

Brown, Hugh B. "Conference Talks," *The Improvement Era,* LXVI, (December, 1963), p. 1058.

Buttrick, George A. *The Interpreter's Bible.* New York: Abingdon-Cokesbury Press, 1952.

Cain and Abel. Cathedral Film Strip. Old Testament. Series one.

Carter, Kate B. (comp.). *Our Pioneer Heritage.* Vol. 8. Salt Lake City, Utah: Daughters of Utah Pioneers, 1965.

Clark, Ed. D., James R. *Messages of the First Presidency.* 3 vols. Salt Lake City, Utah: Bookcraft, 1965.

Clark, J. Reuben. *On the Way to Immortality and Eternal Life.* Salt Lake City: Deseret Book Company, 1953.

Cowley, Matthew F. *Wilford Woodruff.* Salt Lake City: Bookcraft, 1964.

Dummelow, Rev. J. R. *A Commentary on the Holy Bible.* New York: MacMillan Co., 1949.

Fallows, Rt. Rev. S. *The Popular and Critical Bible Encyclopedia.* Chicago: The Howard Serverance Co., 1905.

Frame, R. M. *The Negro Question,* May 1964, (pamphlet).

Hartman, Louis F. *Encyclopedic Dictionary of the Bible.* New York: McGraw-Hill, 1963.

Hastings, James. *Dictionary of the Bible.* Fifth edition. Edinburgh: T and T Clark, 1903.

Hunter, Milton R. *Pearl of Great Price Commentary.* Salt Lake City, Utah: Bookcraft, 1951.

Holy Bible. King James Version. London: Collins' Clear Type Press, 1959.

Lamb, John. "My Responsibility," *The Improvement Era,* LXIV, (January, 1966), 36-37.

Lee, Rev. J. W. *New Self-interpreting Bible Library.* Chicago: The Bible Education Society, 1922.

Ludlow, Daniel H. (comp.). *Latter-day Prophets Speak;* Salt Lake City, Utah: Bookcraft, 1951.

Lundwall, N. B. (comp.). *The Vision.* Salt Lake City, Utah: Bookcraft Publishing Co.

McConkie, Bruce R. *Mormon Doctrine.* Salt Lake City: Bookcraft, 1966.

Newquist, Jerreld L. *Prophets, Principles and National Survival.* Salt Lake City: Publishers Press, 1964.

The Oxford Annotated Bible. Revised standard edition. New York: Oxford University Press, 1962.

Roberts, B. H. *Comprehensive History of the Church.* Salt Lake City: Deseret News Press, 1930.

Smith, Joseph F. "The Negro and the Priesthood," *Improvement Era.* Salt Lake City: Deseret Book Co. XXXVII (1923-24), 564-65.

Smith, Joseph Fielding. *Answers to Gospel Questions.* 5 vols. Salt Lake City, Utah: Deseret Book Company, 1957-66.

_____. *Doctrines of Salvation.* 3 vols. (Bruce R. McConkie, comp.). Salt Lake City, Utah: Bookcraft, 1954-56.

_____. (comp.) *Teachings of the Prophet Joseph Smith.* Salt Lake City: Deseret Book Co., 1938.

_____. *The Way to Perfection.* Eleventh edition. Salt Lake City: Genealogical Society of The Church of Jesus Christ of Latter-day Saints, 1958.

Smith, Joseph, Jr. (trans.) *The Book of Mormon.* Salt Lake City: The Church of Jesus Christ of Latter-day Saints, 1950.

_____. *The Doctrine and Covenants.* Salt Lake City: The Church of Jesus Christ of Latter-day Saints, 1950.

_____. *Inspired Version: The Holy Scriptures.* Independence, Missouri: Herald Publishing House, 1964.

_____. *History of the Church.* (B. H. Roberts, comp.). Salt Lake City, Utah: Deseret Book Company, 1946.

_____. (trans.). *The Pearl of Great Price.* Salt Lake City: The Church of Jesus Christ of Latter-day Saints, 1959.

Smith, Dr. Wilford S. "Is the Negro My Brother?" (Mimeographed.)

Smith, William. *A Dictionary of the Bible.*

Steward, John J. *Mormonism and the Negro.* Second edition. (Orem, Utah: Bookmark Division of Community Press Publishing Company, 1960.

Strong, James. "Hebrew and Chaldee Dictionary." *Exhaustive Concordance of the Bible.* New York: Eaton and Mains, 1890.

Watt, G. D. (comp.). *Journal of Discourses.* Lithographic reprint of original. Liverpool: S. W. Richards, 1964.

Widtsoe, John A. *Discourses of Brigham Young.* Salt Lake City: Deseret Book Company, 1951.

Young, Robert. *Analytical Concordancw to the Bible.* Twentieth American edition. New York: Funk and Wagnalls Co.